HOW TO TALK TO A MOVIE

Reel Spirituality Monograph Series
SERIES DESCRIPTION

The Reel Spirituality Monograph Series features a collection of theoretically precise yet readable essays on a diverse set of film-related topics, each of which makes a substantive contribution to the academic exploration of Theology and Film. The series consists of two kinds of works: 1) popular-level introductions to key concepts in and practical applications of the Theology and Film discipline, and 2) methodologically rigorous investigations of theologically significant films, filmmakers, film genres, and topics in cinema studies. The first kind of monograph seeks to introduce the world of Theology and Film to a wider audience. The second seeks to expand the academic resources available to scholars and students of Theology and Film. In both cases, these essays explore the various ways in which "the cinema" (broadly understood to include the variety of audio-visual storytelling forms that continues to evolve along with emerging digital technologies) contributes to the overall shape and trajectory of the contemporary cultural imagination. The larger aim of producing both scholarly and popular-level monographs is to generate a number of resources for enthusiasts, undergraduate and graduate students, and scholars. As such, the Reel Spirituality Monograph Series ultimately exists to encourage the enthusiast to become a more thoughtful student of the cinema and the scholar to become a more passionate viewer.

HOW TO TALK TO A MOVIE

Movie-Watching as a Spiritual Exercise

Elijah Lynn Davidson
Foreword by Kutter Callaway

CASCADE *Books* · Eugene, Oregon

HOW TO TALK TO A MOVIE
Movie-Watching as a Spiritual Exercise

Reel Spirituality Monograph Series 1

Cascade Books
An Imprint of Wipf and Stock Publishers
199 W. 8th Ave., Suite 3
Eugene, OR 97401

www.wipfandstock.com

PAPERBACK ISBN: 978-1-5326-1313-5
HARDCOVER ISBN: 978-1-5326-1315-9
EBOOK ISBN: 978-1-5326-1314-2

Cataloguing-in-Publication data:

Names: Davidson, Elijah Lynn.

Title: How to talk to a movie : movie-watching as a spiritual exercise /
    by Elijah Lynn Davidson.

Description: Eugene, OR: Cascade Books, 2017 | Series: Reel Spiritual-
    ity Monograph Series 1 | Includes bibliographical references and
    index.

Identifiers: ISBN 978-1-5326-1313-5 (paperback) | ISBN 978-1-5326-
    1315-9 (hardcover) | ISBN 978-1-5326-1314-2 (ebook)

Subjects: LCSH: Motion pitures—Plots, themes, etc. | Spirituality.

Classification: PN1995.9.R4 D25 2017 (paperback) | PN1995.9.R4
    (ebook)

Manufactured in the U.S.A.   01/11/17

For my parents, Mark and Carrie Davidson
whose insistence that God is bigger than any of us have
the ability to comprehend, so we must pay attention
to other people's perspectives on God, forms the
foundation of my life and the motivation for my work

"in high school our art teacher dragged us "incorrigible little thugs" to the art museum which was showing the classics, including by carvaggio & michel angelo.

at the museum when i was standing in front of a carvaggio piece the teacher walked up next to me and exclaimed how "true, pure & beautiful" the painting was. of course, being a typical 17 yr old idiot, & because i didn't understand, i scoffed.

20 yrs later while watching *The Wire* i finally understood what the teacher actually meant."

NUSRAT5791
commenting on a YouTube video [*sic*]

CONTENTS

REEL SPIRITUALITY MONOGRAPH SERIES
Series Foreword

It is not often that one can speak without hyperbole about the person who "wrote the book" on a given topic. But the truth of the matter is that the Reel Spirituality Monograph Series would not exist if it were not for the theologian and lover of film who quite literally wrote the book on the academic study of theology and film: Robert K. Johnston. His seminal work, *Reel Spirituality: Theology and Film in Dialogue*, has shaped the imaginations (and in some cases, even the careers) of untold numbers of filmmakers, theologians, graduate and undergraduate students, laypersons, and cinephiles alike. The singular influence of this book and its author cannot be overstated, which is why this monograph series has the distinct honor of bearing the name, Reel Spirituality. The series as a whole is dedicated to Dr. Johnston, or as Kutter and Elijah (the series co-editors) know him, our cherished friend and mentor Rob.

Of course, much has changed since the printing of the second edition of Johnston's *Reel Spirituality*, and this is to say nothing of the many upheavals within the film industry and cinema studies that have taken place since the original edition of the book was published in 2000. In the first place, there are hundreds (if not thousands) of new movies released every year (both in the US and globally), which make it difficult for any text on film culture to have a very long shelf life. It is for this reason that Johnston updated and revised *Reel Spirituality* in 2006. But in the past decade, given the increasingly rapid pace at which digital technologies have transformed the whole of modern life, a number of previously unrealized opportunities for storytelling have emerged. The immediate result of this proliferation of digital technologies and distribution platforms has been the blurring of the lines between what constitutes a "film" and other forms of audio-visual storytelling.

What exactly is a "film" anyway? The great majority of movies are no longer even shot on "film," so the term itself is a bit of a misnomer. In addition, a growing number of movies are now premiering exclusively online or simultaneously online and in theatres, so it would be misleading to say that we are concerned only with those audio-visual stories that are created and distributed for theatrical release. And what about the many long-form, serialized stories that are now available on subscription platforms like Amazon, Hulu, and Netflix? These are certainly not "films" in the classic sense of the term, but they are surely on the leading edge of the ever-evolving enterprise we have come to know as the "cinema" (a word that has its origin in the Greek *kinema*, or "movement").

So the Reel Spirituality Monograph Series is indeed concerned with *moving* pictures, but it is crucial to point out that these cinematic images are always already bound up in a shared movement through time and space that involves sounds and words as well. This somewhat expansive notion of the cinema includes "films" as they have been traditionally conceived, but it also makes room for all kinds of moving pictures. It thus generates a form of critical engagement that offers thick descriptions and theologically rich construals of both movies and movie-going in the emerging media landscape. Or to put a somewhat different spin on it, regardless of the final form these narratives assume, our basic contention in this series is that, if followed closely and faithfully enough, cinematic "movements" of various kinds are in fact movements of the human soul.

All this to say, whether a movie debuts in theaters, releases through an online streaming service, or premiers on the indie festival circuit, it is becoming increasingly difficult to distinguish with any sort of clarity what the scope and limits might be for a study of this sort. So rather than try to "rein it in" as it were, we see the blurring of the medium's boundaries as an opportunity to explore the underlying shape and texture not only of the cinema itself, but of the ever-changing culture in which it exists. For this very reason, the various "artifacts" that books in this series explore are wide-ranging—from individual films, to television series, to festival culture(s), to avant-garde cinema.

At the same time, however, we have very little interest in maintaining a slavish commitment to whatever happens to be en vogue at the present moment. In light of how much media is produced every calendar year in the US alone, along with the delayed timetable for publishing books, any attempt to stay "current" would be an exercise in utter futility. But this would also be to mistake the "novel" for the "enduring," which would be its own kind of tragedy. New technologies have indeed created never before seen possibilities for the rapid creation, distribution, and consumption of moving pictures. But they have also opened up a cinematic treasure trove—an untapped reservoir of excellently told stories from every era of film history. Given the ways in which digital technology has granted us access to a seemingly infinite number of films that were once sealed in climate-controlled vaults, the books in this series engage not only recent films, but cinematic "classics" as well, perhaps even favoring the latter over the former.

All told then, one of the larger goals of the series is to contribute to what has become an inherently interdisciplinary and constantly evolving field of study, and to do so in a way that is not only academically rigorous but also capable of responding to new movements that emerge within the discipline from one year to the next. Others have attempted to do this through the publication of various edited volumes. And while these compilations are fine and well, it is often the case that they either lack cohesion (which causes them to be less than helpful resources for scholars and students alike), or feature individual contributions that possess great potential but are left undeveloped. In many instances, certain critical analyses simply require more space than a single chapter will allow, but are not broad-reaching enough to justify a 100,000-word treatment.

The Reel Spirituality Monograph series represents our attempt to find a middle way. In certain respects, what we are doing is analogous to the move many filmmakers are making today—shifting from the constraints of a theatrical exhibition model to the somewhat more liberating model of episodic, long-form storytelling, which has only recently been made possible by the advent of online streaming services. Our goal in making this shift is not only to produce top-flight scholarship by some of the most talented voices in the field, but also to chart a new path for the discipline as a whole. We are thankful to Chris Spinks and the entire team at Cascade Books for partnering with us on this somewhat experimental journey. We hope readers enjoy the unfolding conversation as much as we do.

FOREWORD

If there is one thing we can say about public discourse in North America right now, it's that we have seemingly lost the ability to have meaningful conversations with those who might not see the world in exactly the same way that we do. Whether our differences are economic, political, racial, religious, or otherwise, what's missing from our common life together is a shared commitment to engaging in a mutually enriching dialogue with the other. Given our collective unwillingness to talk with anyone who doesn't look or sound or behave just like us, we have not only become unpracticed at this kind of interaction; it would seem that we no longer have the capacity for it. And if social media feeds or presidential debates are any indication, the result of this conversational impasse is nothing less than a complete loss of empathy.

As Plato would remind us, however, some truths—if not Truth itself—only ever come about dialogically. Which is why, in a cultural context where so much of public life has been co-opted by partisan politics, I find Elijah Davidson's book to be so refreshing and, indeed, important. Davidson has identified one of the few remaining places in the contemporary world where dialogue is alive and well: the movies. Davidson reminds us that, when we go to a movie, we are doing more than consuming entertainment media. We are entering into a conversation. Sometimes it's with a beloved director or cinematographer. In other cases, it's with a particular character or story.

But when film is at its best, these conversations don't stay in the theater. They spill out into coffee shops and living rooms and car rides long after the credits have rolled. That is to say, when it comes to movies, we have found a way to engage in vigorous, passionate, and meaningful debate with fellow filmgoers who completely disagree us. In fact, debating the merits (or lack thereof) of a given film is part of the fun of it all. And yet, we somehow manage to have these impassioned conversations while still remaining friends. Disagreement never dissolves into contempt. Instead, it expands and enriches all parties involved.

To be sure, Davidson's primary concern is to show us how to "talk to a movie" in more constructive, creative, and winsome ways. But in doing so, he also helps us become better conversationalists with each other. And in a time such as this, I can think of no better skill to learn, much less put into practice.

Kutter Callaway

PREFACE

My earliest memory is of standing on the edge of a football field with my mom watching my dad coach the Cross Plains High School football team at practice one afternoon. The sun was setting. The air was hot. My mother was holding my hand. My father was teaching young men how to play the game he loved. More than that—though I didn't understand this until later in life—my father was teaching those young men how to be men of character. For my father, how you played the game was more important than whether or not you won. High school football is a momentary diversion, but the way you participate in it influences the kind of person you become.

My second earliest memory is of being whisked by my mother into our storm cellar to hide from a tornado threatening our tiny West Texas town. I remember we weren't alone. There was someone else with us, but I don't remember whom. I do remember that we were going into the cellar because they were afraid, not because we were. Now, my mother tells me the other couple was a young coach and his wife. She had survived a disastrous storm in Wichita Falls a couple of years prior, known locally as "Terrible Tuesday." In that storm, forty-two people were killed, 1,800 were injured, and 20,000 people were left homeless. She had good reason to be very afraid of tornadoes. We went down into the cellar for her sake, putting her emotional needs ahead of our own.

My third earliest memory is of watching *Raiders of the Lost Ark* with my parents. They have always been movie buffs, and they had rented a VCR and the film to watch on their new, color television. My mother tells me I sat enraptured by the entire film, but I only remember the final scene—spoilers, ahoy—in which angels emanate from the open Ark and kill the Nazis. I remember the Nazi's face melting. I remember being paralyzed with fear while it was happening and then shoving my face into the scratchy, brown fabric of our couch after it was over. I can still smell that couch. My earliest cinematic memory is of being profoundly affected by the power of God as depicted in a movie.

These three events have shaped my life and guided my studies. They have inspired the writing of this book, because they taught me that:

- How we do something is as important as what we do, because how we do it shapes us as people.

- The needs of others take precedence over our own.

- Movies have the potential to communicate the presence and power of God.

In my undergraduate studies at Texas A&M University, I studied Leadership Development and Communication so I could understand how to translate complex topics for a general audience in a way that enables them to put cutting-edge methods into practice in their own lives. In graduate school at Fuller Theological Seminary, I studied intercultural studies in order to understand other cultures and integrate my Christian faith into those cultures. I also

learned how to think and act Christianly toward art. I studied the beautiful complexities of "'Love the Lord your God
with all your heart and with all your soul and with all your
strength and with all your mind,' and 'Love your neighbor
as yourself'" (Luke 10:27). Through my work with Reel
Spirituality, both while a student at Fuller Seminary and
since, I've put all this training into practice helping Christians respond lovingly to cinema, helping them position
themselves to encounter God at the movies.

This little book is a synthesis of those studies. This is a
book about how to watch and respond to movies, because
how we watch and talk about movies matters more than
what we think about them. This method of watching and
talking about movies puts the concerns of the artists who
make the films and the needs of our communities ahead of
our own needs. Also, because we will be responding lovingly and graciously to movies, this method opens us up to
the possibility of hearing (seeing?) God speak to us through
the medium of film.

I work for the Brehm Center for Worship, Theology,
and the Arts, a "center of innovation" at Fuller Theological
Seminary. As such, I am blessed to work with consistently
innovative people. For a time, I had the honor of working with Tina Hamous. Tina was tasked with producing
workshops for Brehm Center to take out of the academy
and into the churches to empower church leaders to put our
worship-arts theory into practice in their congregational
life. Tina helped me develop a workshop on devotional film
criticism. Unfortunately, the workshop series fell victim to
the financial difficulties common to non-profit organizations. I then expanded and refined what we had developed
into this book.

If the world of theological film criticism is a great
house, then this little book is my attempt to crack open the

door for you. If it's a party, this little book is an invitation to join. If it's a National Park, this is the map they hand you as you drive through the front gate. This little book is meant as an introduction to the much wider world of faith and film and a suggestion for how you might go about exploring it.

The only thing original about this book is the particular collection of ideas I have brought together to help you learn how to interact with film. My emphasis on practical application rather than abstract theory is different as well, though not original. I've based my method of application on the work of others, though in all cases their work is on either narrative theory or spiritual development. Many people model this kind of interaction with film, but no one explicates it in an instructive way. Throughout this book—usually at the end of sections—I refer you to more substantial works on each subject. I hope this little book will inspire you to "tour the whole house," "talk to all the party guests," and "venture out onto a trail or two."

The person on whose shoulders I am most obviously standing is Robert K. Johnston—"Rob," as I have known him since the first moment of my seminary career when he welcomed us to his Theology and Film course at Fuller Theological Seminary. Christians have been talking about cinema for as long as there has been cinema, but most writing from Christians has been concerned with what other Christians should or shouldn't watch. The history of Christians and movies is a history of attacks on or defenses of certain films or filmmakers. Rob's book, *Reel Spirituality: Theology and Film in Dialogue*, bypasses this ongoing culture war and realizes a new way to think about cinema. Rob assumes his readers are intelligent, reasonable people, that God is bigger than any of our institutions or ideologies, and that God is as apt to surprise us with divine revelation outside the church walls as in them.

Reel Spirituality is a work of academic theory, but it is a more accessible read than you might assume. Though the first third of this little book does lay the theoretical groundwork for the practical application that follows, and some of that theory is based on what I have learned from Rob, this little book is not a condensed version of *Reel Spirituality*. This little book is one example of the kind of practical application Rob's liberating scholarship makes possible. If you are inspired by what you read in this little book, the first book you should pick up next is *Reel Spirituality*. God only knows what might spark in you as you read it.

The other writer and thinker to whom I am in debt is critic and activist Gareth Higgins. Gareth has never written anything as systematic as *Reel Spirituality*. But he has written reflectively about how movies have shaped his life in *How Movies Helped Save My Soul* and *Cinematic States*. For years he co-hosted the now defunct podcast The Film Talk, on which he argued about current cinema with his co-host Jett Loe. Most recently, he has created and programmed the annual Movies and Meaning Festival. In all cases, Gareth exemplifies an openness to the movies that believes the best of the filmmakers, and he searches restlessly for the film's transcendent import expressed in moments of cinematic grace. In all things, Gareth has modeled a way of interacting with cinema that I hope to make available to you through this little book.

ACKNOWLEDGMENTS

Since this is a book about movies and the potential positive impact they can have on your life, it seems appropriate to me that I would, in this acknowledgment section, note the films and filmmakers that have proven especially beneficial to my life.

So, I must begin by acknowledging Walt Disney (the company, not the man) for their decision to re-release *Beauty and the Beast* in 3D in January of 2012, providing me with the ideal scenario to spend a long day with a beautiful girl I'd recently met whom I knew claimed that movie as her favorite. We watched *Beauty and the Beast* in 3D, talked about it for hours afterward, and I began falling in love with her. She's my wife now. Krista, my love, I'm going to get you that floor-to-ceiling library one day even if I have to write all the books in it myself. I wouldn't have had the discipline or courage to finish this one if not for your ever-present love and support.

Then, I need to acknowledge the philosophical and cinematic ambition of Terry Gilliam. Keep tilting at windmills, sir, because you once felled a celluloid beast called *Time Bandits* and gave my future mom and dad something meaningful to talk about all the way home from the movies. Love broke through for them like a knight through a bedroom wall, they were married, they had me and my siblings, and they instilled in us a faithfulness to God and a love of movies the likes of which could perhaps only be rooted in a movie as God-bothered and imaginative as *Time Bandits*. Mom and dad, I love you dearly.

And I should acknowledge *Angels in the Outfield*, *How the West Was Fun*, *The Sound of Music*, *101 Dalmatians*, and *Babe*, because those were the movies my siblings—Amos, Hannah, Abigail, Rebekah, and Micah, respectively— watched on repeat while we were growing up together. I always wondered why they each loved those particular movies so much, and that put me on a path to trying to un- derstand why and how any of us gain a personal connection to the movies we watch. I always had fun watching those movies (over and over and over again) with y'all, siblings, and I'm grateful I have you all in my dugout waving your arms like you can see something in me I can't and rooting me on.

Damon Lindelof and Carleton Cuse should be name- checked here, too, for their narrative cat-herding duties on *Lost*. Most of the show may have been a smoke screen (monster?) expertly effused to keep the series running, but the hours upon hours of conversation it sparked amongst me and the guys who became my close friends in college were very real. Collectively we are known as the Council of Pie, but individually you are Jonathan Breen, Patrick Gilgour, and Chris Hokanson, and you've all encouraged my writing for longer than doing so was warranted by the quality of the writing. You'll have to have a slice on me next time I make it to Houston.

Becket is an important film, because it was the movie my boss, mentor, and friend Rob Johnston was watching when God shifted his course from engineering to ministry, a shift that led to a lifetime of work pushing people to be open to God in every moment. Reel Spirituality certainly wouldn't exist without him, and I don't know where I'd be if he hadn't taken a chance on me and freed me to use my gifts creatively in service of something greater than myself.

Representatively, I'll acknowledge *Star Wars*, *True Grit*, and *Secret Sunshine* as movies I've had rich conversations about with Joe Gallagher, Kutter Callaway, and Eugene Suen, respectively, my fellow Reel Spirituality co-directors. Working with you all to insist on the value of film in theological education is a joy. Kutter deserves to be singled out in the particular case of this book, because without his embrace of it in its early stages, I never would have had the guts to show it to anyone else much less the grit to find someone to publish it. Thank you, Kutter.

Hmmm . . . I need a film to symbolize the co-joined efforts of a group of people set on encountering God and sharing that life-changing encounter with others, because this book wouldn't exist without Matt Lumpkin, Nick Cannariato, Andrew (A. C.) Neel, Jonathan Stoner, Matthew Aughtry, Avril Speaks, Chris Manus, Katie Poland, Kevin Williams, Todd Johnson, and Tina Hamous, all of whom gave me early feedback on this text and helped me craft it into a better cinematic road map to God. Hmmm . . . *Stalker*! Andrei Tarkovsky's *Stalker* is the movie to acknowledge here, because like my friendship with these fine people, it is life-changing, strangely beautiful, and God-haunted. I'll go into the Zone with y'all anytime.

The Tree of Life is an important film for many reasons, but related to this book, it was the first film I was ever invited to view at a press screening, and all my work is greatly enhanced by my relationships with Jonathan Bock, Corby Pons, Ryan Parker, Andy Peterson, Eric Lokessmoe, and their teams—marketers who connect critics like me with filmmakers. The conversations I recount in the conclusion of this book would certainly have never happened without them. I pray our efforts are always mutually beneficial. I'm grateful for you all.

I need a divisive film—*The Revenant* will work—because I want to thank Josh Larsen, Jeffrey Overstreet, Justin Chang, and Gareth Higgins for treating me like a real critic and encouraging me to keep growing in this profession that is more like a calling since the pecuniary rewards are few. The film I acknowledge here must be divisive, because friendships among critics are contentious—as they should be!—since it is only in the "hermeneutic community" of critics, as Gareth puts it, that films finally reach their true potential. I hope this book creates people who watch, talk, and write about movies with as much intelligence and grace as the four of you watch, talk, and write about movies and live your lives.

I'd like to acknowledge *Field of Dreams* as well, because, "If you build it, he will come," and I am the "you," this book is the "it," and the "he" that came in this case is a "they." The pros emerging magically from my cornfield are Chris Spinks, Matt Wimer, and the rest of team at Cascade books who saw something in my little text and made it into a book. Thank you. I'm not crazy after all.

Finally, thank you, reader, for reading this book. Now turn off your cell phones, open your box of candy, pass the popcorn, and settle in. The overhead lights are dimming, and the lights now flickering on the wall in the front of the room have something to say.

INTRODUCTION

Once upon a time, a young projectionist fell asleep at work. Don't hold it against him. He had already worked all morning cleaning up the theater from last night's screening, he was taking a night class to become a detective, his girlfriend had jilted him in favor of a wealthier guy, and to top it all off, earlier that day he'd been falsely accused of burglary by his girlfriend's father and banished from their house forever. He'd had a hard day. A nap was in order.

Then, something strange happened. While his body slept, the young man's spirit awoke. Bewildered at first, his spirit saw the movie flickering on the screen at the other end of the theater. The actors in the movie looked like the young man's girlfriend, her father, and the cuckolding other man. The plot of the movie resembled the events of earlier that afternoon. The young man's spirit stepped over the frame into the movie, and before the movie ended, his real-life problems were solved.

Once upon another time, some sixty-one years later, though it seems as if only a decade or so has gone by, a young woman living a life very similar to the young projectionist's found herself going to the same movie again and again and again to escape the stresses of her terrible, thankless job and her terrible, philandering husband. She didn't fall asleep, certainly not, for she was enthralled by what she saw on the screen. The characters' lives were so glamorous, so full of adventure. The good people prospered (in time), and the bad people didn't (in time). Everyone who deserved it found true love in the end. Everything on screen made sense, and it all happened exactly the same way every time. Life on the screen was always beautiful, predictable, and full of meaning.

Well, almost always. This time as the young woman watched the actors, she noticed one of the actors watching her. "My god, you must really love this picture," the actor in the movie said, looking directly at the young woman, "You've been here all day, and I've seen you here twice before." "Me? You mean me?" she stammered. Suddenly, the actor stepped off the screen and walked right up to her. He wanted to talk to her, because she seemed to take such delight in the movie. They left the theater together and talked into the wee hours of the night. He was a simple man—he was only a movie character, after all—and he had much to learn about the real world. She was more than happy to answer all his questions and respond with a few of her own.

Neither one of those "once upon a times" really happened, of course. They only happened in the movies— Buster Keaton's immortal *Sherlock Jr.* and Woody Allen's sublime *The Purple Rose of Cairo*, to be precise. But just as the fantastic, fourth-wall-breaking events in each film feel real to the characters, so those movies and many others feel "real" to me. I've never literally stepped across the frame into the movie, but I *have* seen semblances of myself and my friends and family on the screen. I *have* made use of the larger than life events in movies to help me make sense of the more mundane problems in my own life. I *have* looked to the movies for guidance on how I ought to behave in analogous situations. I've never had a movie character walk out into the night air holding my hand—though every time I watch a movie starring Marion Cotillard or Anne Hathaway, I wish one would—but I have felt like movies were asking me questions about the world, inviting my response, and puzzling over me as much as I puzzled over them.

So, I learned how to talk to a movie. I learned how to better understand *what* a movie is saying by learning *how* it says what it says, and I learned how to respond in a way that is consistent with the key principals of my Christian faith—without fear and with humility, generosity, and love. Along the way, I discovered that the conversations I was having with movies were having a deep impact on my life. Talking to movies made movie-watching become more than mere distraction. Watching movies became a kind of devotional practice in which God meets with me in the space between the silver screen, my day-to-day life, and God's word.

I want you to have this experience too, and I don't see any reason why you shouldn't. This book will help you do that. In it, I will teach you how to talk to a movie.

To do this, we will first briefly explore why talking to a movie matters whether you agree with the movie or not. Very often, Christians love movies that they agree with and lambast movies they don't. So much good can come of talking to a movie even if you and the movie disagree. Then, we will figure out exactly what "talking to a movie" is and how it is a way to interact with movies that is, perhaps, prescribed by the book of James. After that, we'll learn about the basic story forms commonly found in movies, the methods movies use to tell those stories, and what those stories accomplish in and through their characters. Finally, we will consider how to make talking to a movie an actual, two-way dialogue that can change your life.

I'll be referencing a lot of movies throughout this book. I'll almost always do so without spoiling any of them. When I'm going to spoil something, I'll warn you first. However, we will be discussing *Raiders of the Lost Ark* in depth. If you haven't seen it, you should watch it before you read this book. Near the end of the book, I include an exercise where you'll get to apply what you've learned to *Toy Story*. You'll need to watch that movie before you do the exercise.

Let's begin.

1

WHY TALKING TO A MOVIE MATTERS WHETHER YOU AGREE WITH THE MOVIE OR NOT

Almost everyone watches movies, though people watch movies for different reasons and with different attitudes. Some people watch movies suspiciously, expecting the movie to persuade them to believe something that is not true. Others watch movies mindlessly, expecting only to be entertained, or rather, distracted from whatever is causing them stress in their life. Others watch movies academically, examining the cinematic techniques being utilized by the filmmakers and criticizing how well those techniques have been applied. Still others watch movies devotionally, expecting the Holy Spirit to meet with them in the dark of the theater via the cinematic medium. Many flit from attitude to attitude while watching a single movie, trying to engage with the movie as completely as possible. However you watch movies, you are engaging with what you are watching at some level.

TALKING TO A MOVIE WILL HELP YOU ENJOY THE MOVIE MORE

Some like to use the word "engagement" to describe the overall attitude of actually paying attention to cultural objects like movies. Engagement isn't passive. It is active. It takes work. Engaged viewers learn the language of cinema in order to better understand what a movie is saying. Then the engaged viewer responds to the movie. If you are an engaged viewer, you will benefit from learning to talk to a movie, because talking to a movie will make you more efficient by helping you better understand and respond to movies. Your engaging work will become better and more fulfilling.

People who do not want to do the work of engaging with movies often say they just watch movies to be "entertained." In this case, engagement is still technically happening. The "entertained" viewer is just letting the movie do all the engaging work. The entertained viewer is going wherever the movie takes her or him. The entertained viewer is in conversation with the movie, because the movie is still talking. The entertained viewer simply isn't saying anything back. If you are an entertained viewer, you will benefit from what you read here as well. You will learn to better understand the language of cinema. You may decide you want to start talking back to the movie. I'm going to try to persuade you to do that. You may remain committed to being entertained throughout. In either case, your movie watching experience will be enhanced.

TALKING TO A MOVIE WILL HELP YOU UNDERSTAND WHAT A CULTURE CARES ABOUT

A good story is fueled by a question. It is a way of exploring "what happens when . . . " Those questions are sometimes unique to a particular culture—Victor Hugo's *Les Miserables* explores what happens when a nation revolts against both political and church authorities, which was a question particular to France in the nineteenth century. Those questions are sometimes more universal—Homer's *The Odyssey* explores what happens when a man leaves his family to go fight in a war and tries to come home again, which is a question humanity has been asking for as long as we have been fighting in wars. Of course, a story need not ask a particular or a universal question. A story can ask both at once. *Les Miserables* also explores universal questions of law and grace; *The Odyssey* also explores the particular religious beliefs of eighth century BC Peloponnesian warriors.

Movies are the dominant storytelling method of our time. Movies are the way we tell stories, the main way we ask "what happens when. . ." *Shane* explores what happens when the wilderness begins to be civilized, which was a particularly American question in the first part of the twentieth century; *Timbuktu* explores what happens when a foreign, radical, Muslim sect takes over an indigenous, moderate Muslim community, which is a particularly North African question in the beginning of the twenty-first century. Those questions reveal what our culture and other cultures care about. Talking to a movie then is a way of listening to the questions a particular culture is asking.

It is important to remember, however, that movies are not always topical. When we start looking for easy analogies to current events in movies, we miss what the movies are saying. Making a movie takes a lot of time, and the hot topics of today likely weren't the hot topics of the day when the movie was written, financed, and filmed. For example, when Pixar's *WALL•E* was released in theaters in 2008, many people saw it as blatant propaganda for the environmental movement. After all, *WALL•E*'s story centers around saving the planet from over-pollution via a tiny plant growing in a work boot, *An Inconvenient Truth* had recently won the Oscar for Best Documentary in 2007, and the environment was a consistent issue in the 2008 presidential election. However, writer/director Andrew Stanton first conceived of the movie—including the fact that the earth is covered in garbage and that our robot hero finds a single living plant—in 1994, long before the current environmental movement was winning Oscars and being debated by presidential candidates.

Talking to a movie helps us understand what a culture cares about in the broad sense on the thematic and philosophical level. Rarely is a movie talking about current events. Current events might resonate thematically with movies, but it's the themes that matter, not the events themselves. Both *WALL•E* and the environmental movement are concerned with how we should best care for what we love, be that a friend, a romantic partner, or the planet.

TALKING TO A MOVIE PREPARES YOU TO TALK TO OTHER PEOPLE ABOUT THINGS THAT MATTER

Because movies are concerned with the questions that concern cultures, it is likely that your family, friends, neighbors, and co-workers are concerned about those things too. Talking to a movie prepares you to talk to other people about those questions, and talking to each other has the potential to effect real change in our relationships and our world.

Movies are a safe subject of conversation that can lead to weightier matters. Here are two examples of this dynamic from my own life.

Once during dinner at a work function, I began talking to a recent acquaintance about *Skyfall*, the James Bond movie from 2012. We were discussing the ways *Skyfall* represents a reset on the James Bond franchise, bringing it back, in many ways, to where it was in 1963. We also discussed the subtle ways it develops the James Bond character, particularly in suggesting that Bond's sexual history—something essential to the Bond mystique—extends beyond heterosexual norms. This led to a discussion of the ways heterosexuality has been normative throughout Western history and how a more LGBTQ-friendly ethic seems to be spreading throughout contemporary society.

Another time, I was talking to a friend about *Space Jam*, the Michael Jordan/Bugs Bunny mash-up from 1996. We were mainly talking about how much we loved that movie when we were kids and how bad an actor Michael Jordan is in that movie. Then we started talking about how all the characters in the film, heroes and villains alike, are struggling with their vocations or callings, and that led into a deeper discussion about the ways we too struggle with those same questions.

In both cases, the movie began the conversation and, because both my conversation partner and I were skilled in understanding films, the conversation deepened to something more.

TALKING TO A MOVIE POSITIONS YOU TO HEAR GOD SPEAKING TO YOU

Talking to a movie is not simply a process to figure out what a movie means. We're not trying to simplify the films we watch. Talking to a movie is an approach to movies that makes us more aware of the many ways a movie is speaking. Talking to a movie makes us more sensitive to the emotional, intuitive affect of the movie. Talking to a movie makes us more open to irrational realities, including the movement of the Spirit of God in our lives.

God's Spirit often speaks to us through aesthetic experiences such as shared meals, the awesome beauty of nature, or a work of art. Those kinds of experiences go beyond the rational, awakening the intuitive aspects of our being, and the Spirit of God is a being beyond our rational capacities.

Watching a movie passively, suspiciously, or especially with hostility closes you off to these kinds of encounters with God's Spirit. (Though God might still get to you through a movie! After all, the Spirit of God cannot be corralled.) Being willing to listen to what a movie is saying and responding humbly opens you up to these kinds of experiences.

General Revelation is a theological concept that seeks to explain the ways God speaks to people in other forms besides scripture and Christian tradition. Robert Johnston, in his book *God's Wider Presence: Reevaluating General Revelation*, writes:

> When five persons see a sunset and only one of the five experiences God, it is not that the other four are sinfully blocking out the divine from their view, but that the one has been graced serendipitously with the Spirit's revelatory Presence. . . Moreover, when general revelation is described phenomenologically, it is seldom understood as the work chiefly of human reason, but more often as the experience of our imagination. Revelation is something. . . that is primarily located not in reasoning or ethics but in our intuition and feeling. It is not that we by our own

effort conclude or project by rational inference
that God is a reality, but that we receive God's
revelatory Presence in the midst of our lives.[1]

Or, as Jesus says to Nicodemus in John 3:8, "The wind blows
wherever it pleases. You hear its sound, but you cannot tell
where it comes from or where it is going. So it is with everyone born of the Spirit."

Certainly, we cannot command the Spirit of God to
speak to us when and where we please. The Spirit moves
as the Spirit wills. We can only be sensitive to the Spirit's
movements, like a boy scout feeling for the breeze with a
spit-soaked finger. As Johnston writes clearly and as Jesus
implies, detecting the Spirit is a matter of feeling more than
it is a matter of right-thinking. Even "right-thinking" about
a movie cannot guarantee God will speak to you. However,
we can "wet our fingers and hold them in the air" to feel for
the Spirit's wind. Aesthetic experiences can be a great way
to feel for the breeze.

Johnston's book is packed with examples of the ways
God has spoken to people through films. I, myself, have en-
countered God many times in a theater and at home while
watching a movie. Most recently, I was watching *Babette's
Feast*, a charming, challenging Swedish film about a French
cook who gives a great gift to her pious Danish hosts. I had
seen the film before, but this recent time, the Spirit quick-
ened my heart to repent of the ways I've squandered my
gifts and been ungrateful for the opportunities God has
given me to use them. Then, the Spirit extended grace to
me, great comfort and forgiveness, and all within the span
of a two-hour foreign film about French cooking. This is
just one example of a time when God has spoken to me
through a movie.

1. Johnston, *God's Wider Presence*, 23.

TALKING TO A MOVIE WILL MAKE YOU MORE HOSPITABLE

Talking to a movie is a more Christian way to watch movies because it is a more hospitable way to watch movies. *Hospitality* understood most simply is the act of being friendly to strangers—not only to your friends and family—but to people you do not yet know. A work of artistry made by a person is a surrogate for that person. In the case of movies, it is a surrogate for many persons. We should be hospitable to them. The spiritual discipline of hospitality is at the core of what it means to be part of the people of God.

The practice of hospitality by God's people dates back to the patriarch of our faith, Abraham, and carries through as a constant theme of the Old and New Testaments. In Genesis 18, Abraham immediately welcomes in three men only to later learn he is entertaining the Lord himself. The writer of Hebrews references this encounter in admonishing believers to welcome in strangers (13:2). Further along in Kingdom history, when David is hiding from Saul in the wilderness, Nabal refuses to offer hospitality to David and his men, and so David prepares to slaughter the foolish man. Nabal's wife, Abigail, steps in to appease David's anger through the practice of hospitality, and after her husband dies, David takes this hospitable, diplomatic woman as his wife (1 Samuel 25). Also, Ezekiel lists being inhospitable to the poor and needy as the cause of the destruction of Sodom, and Jerusalem's similar sin is cited as the cause for its forthcoming destruction (Ezek 16:49).

In the New Testament, Christ is mendicant and spends his ministry enjoying the hospitality of others. In the famous parable of the sheep and the goats, it is hospitality that separates the faithful from the faithless in the final judgment (Matt 25:31–46). Throughout the rest of the New

Testament, Paul and the other apostolic writers praise those people who extended hospitality to them as they traveled the ancient world declaring the good news of the gospel. Paul and Peter command hospitality in Rom 12:13 and 1 Pet 4:9, and the practice is also held up as a mark of able leadership in 1 Timothy and Titus (3:2 and 1:8, respectively). Furthermore, the book of 3 John consists of a letter commending Gaius for showing hospitality to his Christian brothers. Finally, there are Jesus' words to the church of Laodicea. After chastising them for their inaction and pointing out their complacency in their wealth, Christ says, "Here I am! I stand at the door and knock. If anyone hears my voice and opens the door, I will come in and eat with that person, and they with me" (Rev 3:20). Christ calls the lukewarm Laodiceans back to hospitality.

The importance of offering hospitality to people we do not know is at the heart of the Word itself. The word "hospitality," as used by the New Testament writers, is created by joining two different words—*philos* and *xenos*. *Philos* refers to friends and being friendly. *Xenos* refers to strangers. *Philoxenos* means literally "being friendly to strangers."

Talking to a movie is a way to transform the consumeristic practice of being entertained by movies into a hospitable practice of entertaining the hopes, fears, ideas, and questions of the people who make the movies. The filmmakers are the strangers we are being friendly toward. In her book *Making Room*, Christine Pohl outlines a phenomenal history of Christian hospitality from the days of the first Christians to today. I suggest, to talk to a movie is to participate in this long tradition of Christian hospitality.

Throughout the New Testament, when the apostles write of showing hospitality, they are exhorting their readers to welcome in people unknown to them. Most often, they seem to be referring directly to traveling Christians who were far away from their homes and without means to tend to themselves. In a world where declaring oneself a follower of Christ could very likely mean martyrdom, a hospitable household was the difference between life and death. In addition to opening homes to itinerant preachers, early Christians also welcomed in the poor, marking their communities as exceptional among their contemporaries. Talking to a movie is a similarly exceptional and counter-cultural way to interact with cinema today.

In the Constantinian period, the practice of hospitality gave birth to the establishment of hospitals and was termed "public service." The leaders of the day urged Christians not to forget that hospitality was an individual discipline as and not just a work of the organized church. It is not only for institutions like Fuller Seminary (whom I work for) to be hospitable to movies. It is a calling that we all must heed individually in our regular movie-watching.

Monasteries and abbeys picked up the practice through the Middle Ages, but hospitality was given in varying degrees of quality depending on a person's status, a temptation we are prone to as well if we only welcome in movies that we agree with or that make Christians "look good." The reformers correctly lambasted the established church for using hospitality as a way to welcome in only the rich and powerful, but in response, by relegating hospitality to simply a civic and domestic practice and not a holy one, they stripped hospitality of its status as a common grace due to all people by the people of God.

It wasn't until the last two centuries that the ancient discipline began to be recovered by the Wesleyan traditions and by more contemporary communities like the Catholic Worker movement and various intentional communities, such as the L'Arche Federation and the New Monasticism movement. Talking to a movie is a hospitable practice in step with a similar, new-born insistence on the importance of responding to the arts openly by many Christian arts organizations like Christians in the Visual Arts (CIVA), International Arts Movement (IAM), the University of St. Andrews' Institute for Theology, Imagination and the Arts (ITIA), and Fuller Seminary's Brehm Center for Worship, Theology, and the Arts. Focused on cinema particularly, there is an ever-growing number of websites and podcasts devoted to this sort of interaction with movies. I curate a regularly updated list of links to many of those websites and podcasts on the "Friends" page at ReelSpirituality.com. To make the spiritual discipline of hospitality the guiding principle of your interaction with movies is to join in this long history of Christian hospitality as it continues to grow and develop around the world.

Hospitality is a spiritual discipline with great value to the contemporary church as well, particularly to the church here in the United States. Hospitality extended to the stranger is a transformative act for ourselves, for the stranger, and for our society. This transformative potential is there when we watch movies, and it comes through three main areas.

First, the discipline of hospitality affords us the opportunity to meet Christ. In the parable of the sheep and the goats, Christ praises and condemns people based on their treatment of the poor, the imprisoned, the sick, and the stranger (Matt 25:31–46). Christ identifies himself as the mendicant among us, and our treatment of the least becomes our treatment of our Lord. Indeed, hosts often find that they are blessed beyond the blessing they provide to others, as should be expected when one is welcoming Christ into one's home. Christine Pohl writes, "[When we are oriented to seeing Jesus in the guest], we are more sensitive to what the guest is bringing to us, to what God might be saying or doing through her or him."[2] This cannot be overemphasized. The purpose of any spiritual discipline is to put us in contact with and draw us closer to God, and hospitality brings us physically face-to-face with our Lord. Being hospitable to movies prepares us to meet Christ in the movie theater.

Secondly, particularly in the United States, in contrast to the practitioners of hospitality in the early churches and in the church today in much of the rest of the world, we have an abundance of material wealth. Christ's words to the Laodicean Christians ring especially true in North American Christian ears. "I know your deeds. . . you are lukewarm," Christ says, "You say, 'I am rich; I have acquired wealth and do not need a thing.' But you do not realize that you are wretched, pitiful, poor, blind, and naked." After urging them to lay aside their wealth, Christ tells them that he is knocking on their door and offering them the opportunity to host (Rev 3:15–20). Similarly, when the rich young ruler expresses his desire to follow Christ, Jesus tells him to give what he has to the poor and then come and be his follower (Matt 19:16–22).

Wealth so easily becomes our identity. Some of us even root part of our identity in how many movies we've watched, as if by watching them, we own them. Practicing hospitality becomes a means of giving ourselves away, humbling ourselves, and expressing gratitude to God for his care for us. Rather than resting in our abundance, we are called to use our wealth to help others that thanksgiving may be brought to God (2 Cor 9:11). Hospitality is a discipline of noticing God's grace in our lives and offering that grace to others. Hospitality is humbling to the host. It positions us rightly toward God and toward other people whom we are called to love.

2. Pohl, *Making Room*, 68.

Finally, the discipline of hospitality establishes the kingdom of God in our world today. As stated before, hospitality, at its most fundamental level, as extended to strangers, promotes inclusion and equality. This is why it is so important to welcome in strangers. Friends and family members are, for the most part, already on equal footing with their host. Outsiders are not. As true hospitality humbles the host, it also elevates the guest. Christ's kingdom is one in which "there is neither Jew nor Greek, slave nor free, male nor female" (Gal 3:28). All are equal. Also, God has a history of commending the equal treatment of the outsider. In Leviticus, God exhorts the Israelites to love the alien among them as themselves because they were once aliens in Egypt (19:34). Because of Christ's work on the cross and by rising from the grave, love is available to all. Love isn't foreign anymore. Hospitality is how we extend that love to others. Watching movies hospitably is a way of extending love to the people who made them. It establishes the kingdom of God in the movie theater and in our living rooms.

Nowhere is this kingdom-establishing potential more evident than in the Eucharist, in which Christ performs the ultimate act of hospitality—he literally offers himself for our sustenance. Christ invites all to sit at the table as equals and feast on him. As members of the Body of Christ, when we discipline ourselves in hospitality, we become the Eucharist—we offer ourselves to the world.

When you sit down to watch a movie, you are welcoming in a stranger. Again, the entertainment paradigm becomes the most appropriate to call upon, but instead of being entertained *by* the movie, the viewer is the one doing the entertaining. To watch a movie is to entertain it and, by proxy, the people who made it. It is an act of hospitality, or at least it can be if it is done with openness, grace, and a self-sacrificial spirit.

Once again, read Christine Pohl's book *Making Room: Recovering Hospitality as a Christian Tradition f*or a thorough exploration of the historical discipline of hospitality if you are interested in learning more about this faith-shaping practice which applies, of course, to much more than movie-watching.

SUMMARY

In summary, talking to a movie will help you enjoy the movie more, clue you in to what a culture cares about, spark interesting conversations with other people, open you to the movements of God's Spirit, and make you more hospitable. So, why wouldn't you want to talk to a movie? Let's learn how.

2

LEARN TO LISTEN FIRST
AND THEN RESPOND

A conversation happens when someone speaks and then someone else listens and responds. Too often, we Christians are too eager to speak about and against movies without listening to them. Sometimes we do this without even seeing a movie first, much less seeking to understand what it might be saying.

This tendency is understandable. We look at the world, and we see a place increasingly hostile to our faith, a world *for* the very things we are *against*. It's as if our culture read the Bible's list of the fruits of the Spirit—love, joy, peace, patience, kindness, goodness, gentleness, faithfulness, and self-control—and chose lust, despair, violence, greed, cruelty, malice, callousness, selfishness, and overindulgence instead. Movies appear to be built upon a foundation of those nine vices, and they seem to make those vices attractive. We fear that movies are winning the hearts and minds of our culture for evil. So we get angry, and we rail against the movies, those "tempters" who are leading our society astray.

We forget what James teaches. He writes, "Each person is tempted when they are dragged away by *their own* evil desire and enticed; they are lured away and enticed by them" (1:14, emphasis mine). The temptations come from within us, not from without. When we watch a movie and feel desire for evil things begin to grow within us, it's because like the characters on-screen, we too are inclined toward sin. The moral choices the characters in movies face, we face, though usually in much less intense circumstances. Lust, despair, violence, greed, cruelty, malice, callousness, selfishness, and overindulgence are facts of the characters' worlds just as they are facts of ours. What matters is how they and we respond to those vices.

Once you learn to talk to a movie, I think you'll be surprised to discover that most movies support the kind of moral framework for life that Christianity supports. We'll touch on a lot of movies that do this throughout the rest of this book. Most movies are on the side of good, or at least they want to be. When they are on the side of good, we can credit that goodness to God and thank God for it. As James also writes, "Every good gift, every perfect gift, comes from above. These gifts come down from the Father, the creator of the heavenly lights, in whose character there is no change at all" (1:17).

"Character" is a key word to note in that verse. God's character doesn't change, but human character does. Movies are chiefly concerned with character change. Characters change from bad to good, from good to better, or bad to worse over the course of the movie. In learning how to talk to a movie, you are going to learn how to understand that character change and respond to it.

But before we can talk to a movie, we have to learn to listen to it. James helps us again. He isn't writing about movies, of course, but he is writing about how Christians ought to interact with the world. He writes, "Everyone should be quick to listen, slow to speak, and slow to grow angry. This is because anger doesn't produce God's righteousness. Therefore, with humility, set aside all moral filth and the growth of wickedness, and welcome the word planted deep inside you—the very word that is able to save you" (1:19–21).

We are supposed to listen first and listen well, then speak, and seldom become angry, because anger isn't helpful. Then, after we have listened, we are supposed to humbly push aside what is bad and welcome what is good—the word of God already in us. When we listen and humbly respond, God's good in us sprouts up, and we are close to salvation. When we watch a movie, we need to listen to it, temper any anger, humbly set aside what is bad in the movie, and embrace what is good, listening to our own hearts to hear the good placed in us by Christ reverberating at the good we hear in the movie.

We're not done yet though. It is not enough to simply cheer the good we discover in movies. We are not called to be merely lovers of good. James tells us to put it into action. He continues:

> You must be doers of the word and not only hearers who mislead themselves. Those who hear but don't do the word are like those who look at their faces in a mirror. They look at themselves, walk away, and immediately forget what they were like. But there are those who study the perfect law, the law of freedom, and continue to do it. They don't listen and then forget, but they put it into practice in their lives. They will be blessed in whatever they do. (1:22–25)

17

We have to take what we learn and put it into practice in our lives, and we have to continue to do this. It's not a one-time shot. Talking to a movie is a way of watching a movie with an ear to what God might be stirring inside us. It is a spiritual discipline, a way of attuning ourselves to the good work the Holy Spirit is already doing in our lives and participating in that work by being obedient to the Holy Spirit's direction after we leave the theater.

3

WHEN WE DON'T LIKE
WHAT WE HEAR

The first things many Christians see (or hear) when they watch movies is the movies' explicit content. Many Christians want to know how much profanity, violence, sex, and nudity are in a movie before they will see it. Much of this concern stems from a desire to "guard" our hearts (Prov 4:23) and to "be holy" (1 Pet 1:15). Much of this concern over explicit content also stems from a desire to protect our children from images they are too immature to handle. We recognize that movies are very skilled at making us feel things. In both cases, we are trying to moderate our feelings or the feelings of those in our care lest we be incited to sin or emotionally disturbed by what we see and hear in movies.

Movies are certainly emotionally evocative. The basis of this book is built on the belief that cinema is capable of stirring up thoughts and emotions in the audience. Filmmakers make movies for this purpose.

However, it is important to understand that movies don't create emotions. They provoke what's already there. Movies can show us what someone unlike us feels, but unless we recognize ourselves and our stories in the characters and their stories, that knowledge is purely factual. When we go a step further and identify with the characters—seeing ourselves in them—that's when our emotions are stirred. The emotions were already ours. Any temptation to sin that accompanies those stirred emotions was already ours too. The movie just made us aware of it, as covered in more detail in our look at the book of James in the previous chapter.

Regarding protecting ourselves and our children from harmful content—yes, we should be careful what we watch. We have to be aware of our own emotional capacities and the capacities of the people for whom we are responsible. But we should also be growing in our abilities to understand our emotions as guides toward proper love of our neighbors and worship of God. Movies provide this opportunity to grow in this way.

So when we watch a violent film and feel excited by the villain's demise, we should likely be both encouraged in our own campaigns against evil in our world and repentant of our bloodlust, since vengeance of this kind belongs to God, not humanity. We should mourn that it is not yet possible for all men and women to be reconciled to one another. We should ask God to work peace in our world.

When we hear profanity or coarse speech in movies, we should listen for brokenness that motivates these characters to express themselves so vehemently. We should consider the real people the characters are based upon and why they feel the need to speak abrasively. People curse to get attention. What are they trying to get us to notice?

When we feel aroused by sexuality in films, we should praise God for creating this mysterious physical drive that draws us to each other. We should thank God for making men and women beautiful to behold. We should ask God to help us see women and men's full humanity instead of reducing them to solely their sexuality. We should repent of our desires to possess others when we have been commanded to give ourselves up for them.

This way of responding to explicit content in movies is a further outworking of placing hospitality at the core of our movie-watching ethic. If we are merely being entertained by movies and consuming them, of course we want to be careful about what we ingest. But if we are seeking to have a conversation with a movie about what matters in life, we'll interact with movies very differently. We will be more forgiving and more gracious. We will not approve of everything we hear or see, but just as we wouldn't write a person off simply because they use coarse speech, we won't write off a movie simply because its manners aren't as refined as ours. And just because a movie uses profanity or violence or sexually explicit images doesn't mean God isn't able to use that movie to speak to you, just as God is still at work in the lives of people who cuss and tell "dirty" jokes.

For most of my life, I obeyed an extremely strict ethic concerning what I would allow myself to watch. Before I watched any movie, I researched its content and would close my eyes and ears whenever scenes arrived that I already knew contained explicit content. Often, I even left the theater or the room entirely until one of my friends or family members called me back in once the scene was over. I was like Paul—"with respect to observing the law (which I had established for myself) a Pharisee. . .with respect to righteousness under [my] law, blameless" (Phil 3:5–6). I refused to let what I heard or saw in movies corrupt my mind.

Then I learned that movies were the work of people asking questions about the world and God and humanity's relationship with both. I realized that my neighbors and friends who were watching those movies were doing so in large part because they too had questions about the world and God and their relationship to both. I knew that Christ wanted me to love those people, to be in relationship with them, and to talk with them about the questions they have. And I knew that, as Paul wrote, "In Christ I have a righteousness that is not my own and that does not come from [any law] but rather from the faithfulness of Christ" (Phil 3:9). I didn't have to maintain my righteousness by avoiding sex scenes in movies. My righteousness is maintained by Christ.

A little later in Philippians, Paul writes this, which has become one of my guiding texts for interacting with media of all kinds:

> Be glad in the Lord always! Again I say, be glad! Let your gentleness show in your treatment of all people. The Lord is near. Don't be anxious about anything; rather bring up all your requests to God in your prayers and petitions, along with giving thanks. Then the peace of God that exceeds all understanding will keep your hearts and minds safe in Christ Jesus. (Phil 4:4–7)

Free from the fear that what I heard or saw was going to corrupt me and happily secure in the Lord, I was able to interact with movies with a gentle spirit absent of anxiety or hostility. When something bothers me, I pray that Christ will guard my heart and mind as he has promised. I have had such peace since I learned to happily rest in God's care for me.

Paul continues:

> From now on, brothers and sisters, if anything is excellent and if anything is admirable, focus your thoughts on these things: all that is true, all

that is holy, all that is just, all that is pure, all that
is lovely, and all that is worthy of praise. Practice
these things: whatever you learned, received,
heard, or saw in us. The God of peace will be
with you. (Phil 4:8–9)

Rather than focusing on the "bad" things in movies, I
began focusing on the "excellent" and "admirable" things.
Rather than closing my eyes and ears and leaving the room
when I watched movies, I began watching and listening for
any true, holy, just, pure, and lovely things. I was surprised
to find them in many of the movies and scenes I had refused to watch before. In art, darkness and light are often
found side-by-side, because artists know that placing them
in relief of one another makes their presence and nature all
the more clear. And I began trying to put the good things
I saw in movies into practice in my life instead of merely
letting them pass by. I have experienced a peace in my
interactions with media that I never knew when I was so
concerned with avoiding explicit content at all costs.

It can also be difficult to understand what a movie
means when it uses violence or profanity or sexuality to say
what it is trying to say without learning a little bit about how
the language of movies—cinematography, editing, scoring
and sound design, genre, and acting—works. Learning how
to talk to a movie will help you better hear what a movie
is saying no matter what kind of "language" it uses. Sometimes, the content of "clean" movies is more troubling than
the content of "dirty" ones.

Ultimately, your ethic of interacting with explicit
content in movies is up to you. No one will or can force
you to see or hear anything you don't want to see or hear.
Whatever your decision on this subject, do what you do
with a clear conscience and secure in the knowledge that
"the Lord is near . . . and the peace of God that exceeds

all understanding will keep your hearts and minds safe in Christ Jesus."

I imposed an ethic of avoidance upon myself when I was a child. It was not imposed upon me by my parents or my community, so it was easier for the Holy Spirit to move me toward a more open posture toward films. I didn't have to break communal ties to act hospitably toward films. If you come from a more dogmatic culture and need help feeling free to engage with less "family friendly" movies, check out Jeffrey Overstreet's book *Through A Screen Darkly*, a "memoir of dangerous moviegoing." Many people have found Overstreet's book helpful.

4

LEARNING TO LISTEN

The best method I have found for beginning a conversation with a movie that has the potential to be spiritually enriching is to understand basic story structure in movies, the way that structure provides an opportunity for characters to change for the better, and the methods filmmakers use to communicate that structure.

Most movies work in similar ways. Most filmmakers tell similar stories using similar techniques with varying degrees of success. Listening to a movie is about learning to "hear" (really, *see*) types of stories and common techniques. It's about looking for and recognizing patterns in cinema.

As such, watching a movie and responding to it is an intuitive process. As Massimo Pigliucci writes in *Answers for Aristotle: How Science and Philosophy Can Lead Us to a More Meaningful Life*, "At bottom, intuition is about the brain's ability to pick up on certain recurring patterns."[1] Then, we determine meaning based on those patterns.

1. Pigliucci, *Answers for Aristotle*, 94. I am grateful to Maria

25

When we watch a movie, or interact with any other form of art actually, we locate meaning in the connections we make between the parts of the whole. A work of art is a thing in itself, but it is also a collection of things. An artwork is a collection of brush strokes or a series of musical notes or a combination of dance steps choreographed together. An artwork is also part of a stylistic movement, an entry in the work-life of the artist, and part of the greater culture out of which the artwork has come. In the case of movies, the artwork is a series of lit shots edited together, commonly overlaid with music, and most often done so in order to tell a story.

You may be thinking, "But I don't 'get' art, and I'm not an intuitive person." Everyone operates intuitively to some degree, and everyone can develop their intuitive ability in a particular area of interest. You already do this for things you do regularly in life. You don't have to think about every step of your bathing process. You don't drive a car by reciting to yourself the rules of the road in every moment. You aren't having to rationally connect each letter and each word to each other in this sentence to read it. That's because, by much practice, those activities have become intuitive processes for you. Pigliucci continues, "Intuitions get better with practice—especially with a lot of practice. . . . The more we are exposed to a particular domain of activity the more familiar we become with the relevant patterns (medical charts, positions of chess pieces), and the more and faster our brains generate heuristic solutions to the problem we happen to be facing in that domain."[2]

So, you *can* learn to recognize common patterns in movies. With practice, you can develop those intuitive

Sharapova at Brain Pickings (https://www.brainpickings.org/) for pointing me to this book.

2. Ibid.

mental muscles. Learning to talk to a movie will give you a head start on knowing which patterns to look for in the movies you watch.

Once we have recognized those patterns and "heard" what a movie is saying, we can recall Scripture and the active work of God's Spirit in our lives, look for ways in which the movie and our faith correspond and contradict with each other, and respond. In this way, listening to a character's arc stretched over a movie's structure provides the opportunity for us to respond to what God might be saying to us through the movie.

5

BASIC STORY STRUCTURE

The first step to learning how to talk to a movie is to learn basic story structure. Most movies stick to a simple plot pattern. You are probably already aware of the parts of this pattern even if you don't know exactly how to label them. They are the parts of the narrative arc that you likely learned in your high school English class. Movies arrange them in a predictable way based on time, because everything in a movie happens on the clock. This pattern is:

- The Prologue

- The Problem

- The Rising Action

- The Climax

- The Resolution

Let's look at each of them one at a time briefly. For a much more in-depth discussion of the parts of a story specifically in movies, read Robert McKee's *Story: Style, Structure, Substance, and the Principles of Screenwriting*—a great book about how audiences interact with stories written as a primer on Hollywood screenwriting form.

Throughout this section, I'm going to refer to *Raiders of the Lost Ark* for examples of each part. If you haven't seen the film, you should stop reading and watch it. It's a lot of fun, incredibly popular, and I'm going to completely spoil it for you if you haven't already seen it.

THE PROLOGUE AND THE PROBLEM

The Prologue

The prologue is the first fifteen to twenty minutes of a movie. During this time, we meet our main character(s) and learn what life looks like for her or him. Usually, the character is pretty happy with life, or at least she or he is unaware that things could be different than they are right now as the story we are seeing begins.

One of my college professors contended that the opening credits and first fifteen minutes of a movie was all that was necessary for understanding a movie. She claimed that if we understood that part, we'd understand everything that came after. She perhaps overstated a little, and her theory cannot account for movies whose method is to frustrate audience expectations, but the first fifteen minutes is indeed essential for following along with the rest of a movie. As you are aware, if you miss the first fifteen minutes of a movie, you might as well not watch it at all, while if you miss as much as half an hour in the middle, you'll probably still enjoy the ending.

During the prologue, we also learn how the main character(s) needs to change. Either she believes something wrongly, has a glaring character flaw, or she needs to learn something new. As we will learn at the climax, this moral or psychological need is greater than whatever material thing the character wants, and the character will mature only if she fulfills this moral or psychological need.

This thing that a character needs to learn is what the movie truly cares about. How the character resolves this need reveals to us what the movie believes. This is why a movie that looks very un-Christian on its surface can actually be very Christian underneath. For example, Martin Scorsese's *The Wolf of Wall Street* features three hours of moral debauchery. Its characters curse constantly, abuse drugs and alcohol with abandon, engage in sexually depraved activities, commit all sorts of crimes, and get away with it. The movie depicts all of this in extremely explicit ways. However, *The Wolf of Wall Street* is ultimately about how its characters need to see the error of their ways. We learn in the first few minutes that their greed has led them into this kind of life, and for the next three hours of movie-time, they are given opportunity after opportunity to repent. *The Wolf of Wall Street* is as morally upright as what Paul writes to Timothy in 1 Timothy 6.

In the first few minutes of *Raiders of the Lost Ark*, we learn that Indiana Jones is an archeologist-treasure hunter, he does not respect the power of gods, he's good at getting out of tricky situations, he doesn't get to keep what he is searching for, and he sees women as distractions from his professional pursuits. We learn all of this before we even hear the word "ark."

Remember, the things a character believes in the beginning of film are the wrong things (most often), and the events of the story are the method by which she or he gains wisdom. So, from *Raiders of the Lost Ark*'s prologue, we can see that 1) people should respect god's power, and 2) people should value relationships over work. The rest of the film depicts Indy learning those two things.

The Problem

Fifteen to twenty minutes into most movies, the character(s) is presented with a problem. She or he spends most of the rest of the movie trying to solve that problem. (You'll often see this point in the story referred to as the "conflict." I don't like that term, because most movies feature multiple conflicts on multiple levels. Indiana Jones already has two conflicts—not believing in god and valuing work over relationships—before he is even aware of the movie's problem.) The problem in a movie is external, explicit, and the character(s) is aware of it. Put simply, the problem is the thing the character wants to obtain or achieve.

Often the problem is a tangible object, like the Ark in *Raiders of the Lost Ark,* or a lot of money in *Ocean's 11.* More often, the problem is intangible, though it is still the explicit goal of the character. Solving a mystery is a common intangible problem, as Jason Bourne has to do in *The Bourne Identity*, or "getting home," as Marty McFly has to do in *Back to the Future.* Whether tangible or intangible, the movie's plot revolves around the main character(s) trying to get that thing. Alfred Hitchcock coined the term "MacGuffin" for the problem that fuels the action of the movie. The MacGuffin is the thing all the characters want, but it's not ultimately what the movie is about.

How the character reacts when the problem is presented to them is a result of that character's deeper desires. Different characters would respond to the same problem in different ways. As an archeologist, Indiana Jones's deeper desire is to discover the truth, so he looks for clues, follows leads, and solves puzzles to find and obtain the Ark of the Covenant. Indy's rival, Belloq, doesn't care about the truth at all. He just wants the power and esteem that would come with possessing the Ark. (Notice how both he and Indy each react to getting ahold of the idol in the film's prologue—Indy is content with having found it and gives it up when he needs Satipo to throw him the whip; Belloq holds the idol aloft so that the South American natives bow down before him.)

There are nine deeper desires different characters in movies might be trying to achieve. They are:

1) Maintaining Honor

Characters whose deeper desire is to maintain honor are committed to doing right in every circumstance. They are women and men of conviction and conscience. Ultimately, they must give up everything, often their very lives, to preserve their honor. *Gladiator*'s Maximus is this kind of character. Actually, many of Russell Crowe's roles fit this category, and sometimes his movies explore the hazards of obeying strict codes, as when Noah in *Noah* and Javert in *Les Misérables* let their sense of right and wrong drive them to commit violent, cruel acts against people they love. On a more feminine, less violent note, *Becoming Jane*'s Jane Austen is this kind of character as well.

2) Finding Love

Characters whose deeper desire is to find love feel a great sense of lack in their lives that they believe can only be filled by earning the love of another person. They go to extreme lengths to become the kind of person someone else might love. Eventually, they must stand up for themselves, actively express their own will, and resolve to be okay even if they are rejected to become more mature. Most heroines and heroes in romantic comedies fit this category. The *Toy*

Story movies are built on this dynamic. Most of Adam Sandler's roles fall into this category as well.

3) Achieving Esteem

Characters whose deeper desire is to achieve esteem pursue success above all else. These characters are consumed with appearances, and they do wrong thing after wrong thing to maintain the appearance of success even though doing so destroys every other aspect of their lives. In the end, these characters have to do the right thing even though it cost them everything, if they are going to mature. Tom Cruise became famous playing these kinds of characters in movies like *Risky Business* and *Top Gun*. Cady Heron and The Plastics in *Mean Girls* are these kinds of characters as well.

4) Establishing Truth

Characters whose deeper desire is to establish truth are consumed with a desire for authenticity in all things. They put themselves and their loved ones in danger, both spiritually and sometimes physically, in an attempt to discover the truth in a given situation, the true purpose of their lives, or the true nature of reality itself. Eventually, these characters must accept ambiguity if they are going to survive and find peace. Most detective movies (*Chinatown*, *Vertigo*) and non-James Bond-like spy movies (*The Bourne Identity*, *Mission: Impossible*) are about these kinds of characters as are most movies about artists (*Pollack*, *Ratatouille*).

5) Discovering Order

Characters whose deeper desire is to discover order search tirelessly for the reason and structure that undergirds all of life. They are frustrated by life's apparent meaninglessness. If they are going to be happy, they have to accept that meaninglessness and appreciate what's good in life anyway.

Almost all of the Coen Brothers' films fit in this category as do Wes Anderson's films and "science dramas" like *A Beautiful Mind* (a Russell Crowe outlier) and *The Imitation Game*.

6) Preserving Peace

Characters whose deeper desire is to preserve peace try to remain in the relative safety of what they know. At their core, these kinds of characters are afraid of everything. Eventually, they are forced to face their fear, accept personal responsibility for their lives, and endeavor to achieve something. Coming-of-age movies—like *Juno* or most Judd Apatow comedies—feature these kinds of characters, as do most horror movies, which are essentially coming-of-age movies that make you jump.

7) Having Fun

Characters whose deeper desire is to keep having fun are deeply selfish characters. They don't want to be limited by any other person, institution, or demand on their lives. They eventually have to admit that they have a responsibility to society as a whole, and they have to do something to benefit all humankind. These characters' moment of maturation is typically subtle. Sometimes they appear to have no character arc at all. James Bond is the preeminent example of this kind of character. Wayne and Garth from *Wayne's World* fit in this category as well.

8) Gaining Power

Characters whose deeper desire is to gain power value strength and influence above all else. These characters don't care if they appear successful or not as long as they are in charge. These characters are always ready for a fight, and they reach maturity if they stand up for someone weaker than themselves at great cost to themselves. This usually happens after they encounter innocence. *Citizen Kane*'s Charles Foster Kane and *The Godfather*'s Michael Corleone fit into this category. On a more hopeful note, Erin Brockovich and Joan of Arc fall into this category as well.

9) Avoiding Conflict

Characters whose deeper desire is to avoid conflict just want to be left alone. They want to stay home and stick to their routines. Something disrupts their normal life, and they face a constant temptation to turn around and go home prematurely. They have to see the journey through even if it means never going home again. *The Hobbit*'s Bilbo Baggins is stereotypical of this kind of character. Many of the roles that made Tom Hanks famous are this kind of character as well (*Joe Versus the Volcano*'s Joe, Forrest Gump, Captain Miller in *Saving Private Ryan*, and *Cast Away*'s Chuck Noland, to name a few).

Overall, we could also refer to these problems and deeper desires as *temptations*. Characters pursue these things at the peril of their souls. Indiana Jones's desire to get the Ark and learn the truth about it directly conflicts with his needs to respect the power of God and value relationships over work. Once again, by the climax of the movie, the characters are going to have to abandon both the object they are chasing and their deeper desire if they are going to mature.

A thorough investigation of these nine temptations, applied not to movies but to our own spiritual lives, can be found in Richard Rohr and Andreas Ebert's great book *The Enneagram: A Christian Perspective*. As someone preoccupied with character development in movies and interested in personality inventories, Rohr and Ebert's book has become my go-to resource for spiritual development.

Laurie Hutzler's Emotional Toolbox Screenwriting method, which appears to be based in part on the enneagram among other personality inventories, has also been helpful to me as I've learned more about character development in movies.

Questions to Ask During the Prologue and Problem

1) Who is/are the main character(s)?

2) What does s/he believe about the world?

3) What is incorrect about that belief?

4) What is the movie's problem?

5) What is the character(s) chasing?

6) Why does s/he want it?

7) What does this reveal about her/his character?

8) What are her/his deeper desires?

9) What will maturity look like for this character?

RISING ACTION

The rising action commands the bulk of the movie. It will last for the next hour to hour and a half after the problem is first presented to the main character(s). During this part of the movie, the characters will encounter obstacle after obstacle that they must overcome in order to achieve their goal. At the same time, they will be given opportunity after opportunity to see the error of their thinking, lay aside their temptations, and embrace maturity. But the characters will not take advantage of those opportunities.

In *Raiders of the Lost Ark*, Indiana Jones solves puzzle after puzzle and survives action sequence after action sequence as he chases the Ark. The Ark stays always just beyond his grasp. He continually rejects any suggestion that the Ark is anything other than an historical object, that it might be evidence of God's power, even though his perpetual escapes from danger are nothing short of providential. He also continually rejects Marion, the woman whom he loves and who loves him, in favor of pursuing the Ark. If Indy were to trust the power of God and choose Marion over work, he could walk away from this problem and live peacefully. God's power would still be unleashed against the Nazis eventually, and Indiana Jones and his friends wouldn't all almost die in the process. The story continues because Indiana Jones refuses to wise up.

MOVIE METHOD

The rising action portion of the movie is an ideal time to look beyond the plot and characters of the movie and at the form of the movie itself. Here, we get to see how the movie is accomplishing its purposes. This method will have been established by the prologue, but the rising action is where it is developed in depth.

At its most basic level, a movie is a series of captured moving images often set to music and/or sound in order to evoke an emotional response. *Cinematography* is the art of composing and capturing the individual images. *Editing* is the art of putting them in series. *Sound design* and *scoring* are the arts of setting those image series to music and soundscapes. How those cinematic elements are arranged grants the movie its meaning or emotional power. *Acting* works in concert with those cinematic elements to embody the emotional impact of the story and provide audiences with an entry point into the narrative. When those cinematic elements are used in similar ways in many films, we call that grouping of films a film *genre*. Identifying a film's genre can be a short cut to understanding what a film is saying. *Casting* works similarly to genre by suggesting what kind of story you are watching based on what is typical of the actors in the movie.

Most often, these elements are used to tell a story. Since story is a means of communication that transcends the cinematic medium, story is usually the easiest way for people to access the emotional power of a movie. That's why I've devoted most of this book to story. Telling the story clearly is the first priority of these cinematic elements in most movies. If they fail to convey the events of the story in a way that the audience understands, they fail in almost all movies.

However, story is not the most subtle or powerful aspect of a movie's communication method. Telling a story is not all that these cinematic elements do. It will benefit us to spend a little time becoming aware of the purely cinematic elements of cinematography, editing, scoring, and sound design and their particular emotional impact; how those things are used by different genres; and how acting functions in films if we want to talk to a movie with greater fluency.

Cinematography

The essence of a movie is that its images move. Strip everything else away—the edits, the sound and color, even representational figures (like the Dot and the Line in the famous Chuck Jones animated short)—and as long as what you are looking at moves, it is a movie. A zoetrope is a movie; so is *Avatar*. The movement in question is both that of the things contained within the image—the characters and objects—and the frame of the image itself. The movement of the objects in the frame and the frame itself convey both narrative and emotional meaning. Put another way, the movement is how the movie says what the movie wants to say. If we want to talk to a movie, we have to be aware of that movement.

The way a movie moves depends upon the perspective that the filmmakers want the viewer to adopt at any point during the movie. Often that perspective is the perspective of a character in the movie. More often, that perspective is the perspective of someone recording the events of the story or telling the tale. Sometimes that perspective is the perspective of someone else entirely who is observing and slyly commenting on what is happening. Perspective often shifts throughout the movie. Most importantly, cinematic perspective is emotional as well as literal. Cinematography is the method by which the filmmakers shift the focus of the image and shift the image itself to get us to feel what they want us to feel throughout the duration of the movie.

An aspect of cinematography besides camera movement that is useful as you listen to what a movie is saying is what film studies refers to as *mise-en-scène*. The term is taken from French theater—French scholars are responsible for much of contemporary film criticism—and it means "the things on stage." In movies, it refers to the things included in the image, everything from props, make-up, and costumes to lighting and even the actors themselves. Cinematic images are constructed, and the things filmmakers choose to make up those images have meaning. Filmmakers would likely never use the term "*mise-en-scène*" on set while making a movie, but they might refer to the "symbolic" intent behind their choices of what to include in their images. In many films, these symbols are layered so expertly it is only upon repeat viewings when you already know the story that you are able to notice how the filmmakers are using "the things on stage" to suggest meaning.

Raiders of the Lost Ark's opening sequence is expertly crafted. As the movie begins, a man rises into the frame. His silhouette fills the sky. We do not see his face. The cinematography keeps us distant from him even as it follows him through the jungle. The cinematography encourages us to ask, "Who is this man?" After a couple of quick incidents that show us he is braver and more capable than the people who are with him, the movie's perspective suddenly shifts. We hear a sound like a twig snapping. A gun! A whip! A man is disarmed and flees afraid. Before we even know who our hero is, we've been granted his perspective. He is smart. He is fast. He is good at getting out of tricky situations. Literally and symbolically, he steps out of darkness and into the light. (The movie plies the symbolism of darkness and light throughout.) Our hero is grizzled and handsome. We don't even know his name yet, but we've been him once, briefly. It was a rush, and we want to be him again.

There is a moral element to this. By encouraging you to adopt various perspectives and feel various ways about what you are seeing, a movie encourages you to interact with the world in a certain way. *Raiders of the Lost Ark* encourages its audience to see the people of South American and African countries as foolish and dispensable. Notice how much smarter the movie's white hero is than his Peruvian guides and the sword-wielding masses of Cairo and how humorously the film depicts their killing. *Raiders of the Lost Ark* also encourages its audience to fear God. Because we identify with Indiana Jones throughout the movie, when he learns that the Ark is more than an artifact, we do too. More than its content, how a movie shows us what it shows us—its cinematography—is where most of a movie's moral value lies.

Editing

The second important tool in the filmmaker's toolbox is *editing*. It is possible to make a movie that is one long continuous recording of events, but those movies are rare, and their style of editing—the total lack thereof—is part of the point. Almost all movies feature edits, sometimes hundreds or thousands of edits, and every edit is either a shift in perspective, as we covered in the last section, or a manipulation of time.

Time is life. Our experience of time passing is the essence of our mortal lives. The ancient Christian idea of eternity is not stepping into "time without end," but rather it is stepping into "God's instant," out of the experience of time altogether, as Charles Taylor explains Augustine in *A Secular Age*.[1] Think of the most blissful moment of your life, when all that had happened before seemed to have led directly to that moment, all that would come after would be impacted by that moment, and time seemed to dissipate completely. That was a taste of eternity, a moment without the experience of time.

Famed Russian filmmaker Andrei Tarkovsky believed that the essence of cinema as an art form is the manipulation of time, our ability to capture moments and "roll [them] and unroll [them] forever." He called cinema a "mosaic made of time." His films are some of the most effective films ever made at making you aware of the ways we experience time as both taxing and transcendent. (Tarkovsky's book *Sculpting in Time* is a fascinating window into both the famed filmmaker's mind and this unique aspect of cinema.)

Movie editing forces you to experience time as the filmmakers want you to experience it. Editing either abbreviates times or elongates it. In a movie, eons can pass

1. Taylor, *A Secular Age*, 57.

41

in an instant (like when the tossed-aloft bone turns into a spaceship in *2001: A Space Odyssey*), or an instant can last for an eon (like when the alarm clock tiles flip to "6:00" for the ten-thousandth time in *Groundhog Day*). Most of the time, edits aren't quite so drastic. They merely speed the story along or slow it down so that we experience important moments more fully.

An editor composes a movie by selecting the most important moments out of all those moments collected while filming. Editing communicates what matters moment by moment and from moment to moment. Editing forces you to stay with a moment or it whisks you away to a new moment. Editing lingers on important things, or it shows important things many times. Unimportant things are either shown briefly or not at all.

Editing also creates meaning by juxtaposing different moments, characters, or objects. A filmmaker might show one person in the fifth century BCE Babylon doing one thing then cut to another person in present day America doing something else to communicate that though these actions are separated by vast amounts of space and time, they are the same. For an example of this, see what D. W. Griffith does in *Intolerance*. A filmmaker might also communicate that though two people are in the same place, they are not "together" by never including them in the frame together. Editing says, "This and this are connected or not connected, either relationally, narratively, or thematically."

For example, in the climactic scene of *Raiders of the Lost Ark*, editors Michael Kahn and George Lucas (uncredited) show us, in this order: Indiana Jones watching the Ark being opened, the Nazis finding nothing but sand inside, Jones's smug reaction to confirming that the Ark is only an artifact and not the resting place of God, and then Belloq's frustration at finding only sand. The editing makes Jones's reaction the most important, since we see it first throughout the scene, and the editing contrasts the reaction of Jones and Belloq. This contrast becomes more important a moment later when God's power emerges and Jones responds with humble contrition—closing his eyes—while Belloq responds with foolish, selfish glee.

As with cinematography, there is a moral element to editing as well. Editing denotes importance. So, when Indy meets up with the swordsman in Cairo and the movie cuts directly from Indy shooting the man to a shot of Marion's basket bobbing through the crowd to Indy resuming his chase without ever showing us the man lying dead in the dirt, the movie is implying, "All that's important is Indy's pursuit of Marion. This man's life is of no consequence other than to show us how much more clever Indiana Jones is than these Egyptians." To be clear, I don't believe Steven Spielberg, Michael Kahn, and George Lucas meant to deprecate Egyptians. It's simply a fact of the way their movie is edited. Movie methods—cinematography, editing, sound design, and scoring—say what they say in their own ways regardless of the filmmakers' intent. This scene in *Raiders of the Lost Ark* would serve as a good reminder to filmmakers to be ever-mindful of what their movie-making method is saying in any moment.

Sound Design and Scoring

Though movies haven't always included audible dialogue and sound effects, movies have always been accompanied by sound. In the early days of cinema, an organist or piano player in the room with the audience played the music live. The music played alongside a film would often differ from performance to performance. Later, when it became possible to encode sound alongside the images on a filmstrip, the music became standardized no matter where or when one saw the film. This music is called the *score* and it differs from the other sounds—*dialogue* and *sound effects*—also encoded alongside the film's images. The combined score and other sounds comprise the movie's *soundtrack*, so called because it was literally a separate track on the filmstrip. As with cinematography and editing, the first job of dialogue and sound effects is to communicate the story efficiently.

There are two types of sound in a film. *Diegetic sound* is sound that comes from within the world of the story. Characters in the story can hear diegetic sound. *Non-diegetic sound* comes from outside the world of the story. Characters in the story can't hear non-diegetic sound. It exists only for the audience. Dialogue, sound effects, and score can all be either diegetic or non-diegetic, and filmmakers like to play with the diegetic location of their movie's soundtrack. For example, near the end of the movie *Birdman*, the arrhythmic, jazz drumming that has dominated the movie's score non-diegetically becomes diegetic when Riggan rounds a corner and we see a drummer pounding on his drum set in the theater kitchen. Now before considering a film's score, let's first consider a movie's dialogue and sound effects.

Dialogue, of course, consists of the words spoken by the characters in the film. Narration is also considered dialogue even though it is rarely spoken by a character visible on the screen. Diegetic dialogue communicates what characters are thinking and feeling about what is happening in the story while it happens. Non-diegetic narration communicates what a character thinks and feels about the story's events at another time. Usually, narration is retrospective—a character is reminiscing about past events—but it can also be from an unspecified time, as when an unborn child comments on the events of Julie Dash's *Daughters of the Dust*. Whether spoken by characters caught up in the story or by characters outside it, always remember that dialogue can't necessarily be trusted. It is simply the characters' perspective on the events of the story. The perspectives of both the filmmaker and the audience are just as valid. Filmmakers often work against the characters to communicate other truths about the characters' situations. The audience is responsible for considering both perspectives and deciding what to accept and reject.

Sound Effects are everything else you hear that isn't dialogue or score. Diegetic sound effects contribute to the filmmakers' creation of a believable world on-screen. Diegetic sound effects are like set decoration or costuming. They can communicate more than setting—a squeaky shoe might indicate a character's awkwardness, for example—but generally diegetic sound effects work to grant the movie's world greater veracity. Like cinematography and editing, when sound effects are added skillfully, you don't notice them.

Often, the absence of expected sound effects is more evocative than their presence. In *Taxi Driver*'s climax, for example, Travis Bickle raids the pimp's row house, guns blazing, to rescue the pre-teen prostitute Iris. Scorsese drains away all other sounds except for the sounds of gun blasts, people screaming, glass breaking, and blood dripping. Bernard Herrman's score is gone as are the otherwise omnipresent sounds of the city. This sound effect mix communicates the movie's feelings about the violence depicted—that is it horrifying—better than any commentary ever could.

Non-diegetic sound effects align more with the movie's score, like a kind of music. They create mood and communicate emotion. Non-diegetic sound effects are relatively rare. Referring to *Taxi Driver* again, in the film's famous "You talkin' to me" scene, the final moment is punctuated by a woman's scream, which has no source in the action on screen. It underlines the horror of the moment. (The scream is actually pulled from the film's climax when Iris screams during the violent finale.)

Here is an example that brings all of this together. The opening scene of *Zero Dark Thirty* consists of the words "The following motion pictures is based on first hand accounts of actual events," followed by the date "September 11, 2001," and then a blank screen and the sounds of people's voices on radios and telephones recorded the morning of the terrorists attacks on Washington DC and New York City on that date. These sounds absent an image prompt the audience to imagine the people whose voices they hear as well as to remember what it was like to live through that morning. The movie wants us to remember the fear we felt that day so that when the next scene begins, and we see a CIA agent torturing a man in order to get information about the 9/11 hijackers, we understand the fear out of which the agent is acting. Before *Zero Dark Thirty*'s narrative even begins, the filmmakers use sound effects and dialogue to 1) situate us in a place and time—September 11, 2001; 2) communicate the characters' emotions—fear; and 3) help the filmmakers influence our emotions as well.

Along with a movie's images, a movie's *score* shares responsibility for telling the movie's story. While a movie's images show you somewhat explicitly the facts of what happens in a story, a movie's score suggests what the movie wants you to feel about what happens. Sometimes this is straightforward, as when *Raiders of the Lost Arc*'s credits roll and John Williams's iconic "Indian Jones Theme" communicates to you that you've just had a triumphant time at the movies (even though you've also just seen the US government disregard the power of God). Sometimes the score works ironically, as in *Nightcrawler*, when James

Newton Howard's score communicates the protagonist Louis Bloom's emotional state at any moment, which isn't necessarily what we are supposed to be feeling about what we are seeing.

Since a movie's score works invisibly, spanning scenes and acts and covering them all under the same sonic blanket, a movie's score provides emotional continuity to the movie that its images would otherwise lack. A movie's images and score work together to give us, the audience, a cohesive audiovisual experience. As Kutter Callaway writes in *Scoring Transcendence*, his book about the potential theological worth of considering film music more seriously, "A film is not a mere aggregate of various cinematic elements; it is a wholly new synthesis that issues from the dynamic interaction between the images we see and the sounds we hear."[2]

Callaway continues by discussing the ways film music is "for" the audience, not the characters on screen. Its score is the way a movie reaches out to us and invites us to respond emotionally to it. The score, Callaway writes, "demands that we avoid purely formal analyses and ask questions concerning the film's reception," which is exactly what we are doing in this book.[3] We are learning how to better receive a movie and interact with it. Read Callaway's book for a more thorough treatment of how to pay attention and understand movie music. For now, just know that a movie's score appeals to your emotions and guides your heart through the story just as the cinematography and editing guide your eyes and the sound design guides your ears.

2. Callaway, *Scoring Transcedence*, 67.
3. Ibid., 71.

Acting

We don't see cinematographers, editors, sound designers, or composers when we watch a movie. We only see or hear their work. If they are doing their jobs exceptionally well, we often don't notice their work at all. We just experience the story they are telling.

But we do see actors. Their work is obvious, so much so, we've even turned what they literally do into a colloquialism for when someone is contributing in their small, particular way to a greater communal work—we say they are "playing their part." *Actors* embody the story's characters and help the audience identify with what is happening on screen.

Screen acting is often contrasted with stage acting. Screen acting is supposedly more subtle and still. Stage acting is supposedly bigger and louder. There is some truth in that comparison, as the use of a camera to capture performances does allow for greater intimacy between the actor and the audience. Screen actors can make small gestures and slight expressions, the camera can catch them, and we can see them projected on a fifty-foot screen.

Furthermore, movies can imply meaning and emotion via the other conventions we have explored (cinematography, editing, sound design, and scoring) and use the actor as a kind of ambiguous surface onto which meaning and emotion can be projected. The movie audience is always (often subconsciously) asking, "What is that person thinking and feeling and why?" We infer answers to those questions based on what is happening to the character in the story, and we are guided along by the movie's other formal conventions. Much of what we think we "know" about a character we actually assume, and the character's actions prove or disprove our assumptions. Our best screen actors are the ones who are most skilled at inviting and playing with who their characters are, what they are thinking and feeling, and what they will do in a given situation.

But screen acting can also be big. Because of the intimacy created by the camera and the screening, and because of the ways filmmakers can emphasize moments, broad emotions can have a greater impact in a movie than they might have in real life. Screen actors convey the emotional state of not just their character, but of the moment in the story as well. Sometimes that emotion is bigger than the character, and it requires a big expression to ring true.

A great example of both of these kinds of screen acting happens at the end of Spike Lee's *School Daze*, a satire about factions of black students at an HBCU (historically black college or university). After two hours of students conflicting with each other over the proper way to be "black" in America, Spike Lee cuts to an empty campus quad as the sun is rising. From far away, Dap (Larry Fishburne) runs down the center of the quad all the way up to the fixed camera until his face fills the screen. Looking directly into the camera, he screams, "WAKE UP!" It is a big moment, because it conveys both Dap's distress at the way his fellow students are fighting with each other and the movie's distress at the way black students are fighting with each other around the country in real life.

Dap continues to scream "Wake up!" as he rings the campus bell, and all the other characters stir in their beds and wander out onto the lawn with him. They all stand around the bell staring blankly. Though the actors do nothing to communicate this, we infer that they have indeed become aware that they need to be as one instead of constantly arguing with each other. Dap has been feuding openly with "Dean Big Brother Almighty of the Gamma Phi Gamma Fraternity" (Giancarlo Esposito), who shows up as well.

Walking through the middle of the crowd, he comes up to Dap, and the two share a look that, though no words are spoken, we take to mean, "We forgive each other and will work together from this point forward." Golden light bathes this scene, and triumphant music plays on the soundtrack, giving emotional weight to otherwise insignificant gestures made by the actors.

Whether the acting is small or big, acting embodies the emotion of the moment in a movie and invites us to empathize with the characters and with the film itself. I am a white man, but when I watch *School Daze*, I feel the tragedy of young black men and women fighting with one another, I long for them to be as one, and I cheer their reconciliation at the film's end. I recognize that they are unlike me, and their struggle is not my struggle—if anything, white men like me are to blame for the existence of this struggle—but I also truly long for peace amongst this group of people. I also understand how I am like them and how, while our particular concerns are different, our emotional drives are the same. We all want both to be free to express ourselves as we see fit and to be unified with one another. Acting provides the entry point for us to experience other people's lives.

In *Raiders of the Lost Ark*, we can see both small and big screen acting happening concurrently in the same scene. In the film's climax as the Nazis are opening the Ark, Indiana Jones and Marion are bound to a stake at the back of the canyon. Harrison Ford can't act big, because he is literally tied up. So, as the Ark is opened, the camera is in tight on his face. We see Ford smirk as the Nazis discover nothing but sand in the Ark. It's a small moment that conveys his great pride. Then, as the angels begin to issue forth from the Ark, his smirk changes into wide-eyed terror. It's another small moment, but in it, we see his pride finally melt away and be replaced by holy fear.

Concurrently, Paul Freeman as Belloq screams first in ecstasy then in horror as the angels begin to swarm the canyon. It's a broad acting moment that morphs into a shocking special effect. The combination of Freeman's acting and the face-melting special effect communicates the scary awesomeness of God's power as well as the danger of blasphemous greed. Both Ford's small moment and Freeman's big moment allow the audience to feel what their characters feel in that moment and caution us against behaving like the characters they portray.

Genre

Identifying a movie's genre can be a shortcut to understanding the way the movie is telling its story. A genre is a grouping of movies based on stylistic conventions. Movies in a genre tend to either use cinematography, editing, sound design, and scoring in similar ways, or they play with those conventions and use them in obviously different ways to call attention to the ways they contrast with other films in their genre.

For example, *Raiders of the Lost Ark* is an action/adventure movie with supernatural/horror elements, so we can expect its story to revolve around motion and exotic locations undergirded by the possibility of paranormal activity. And it does. The story consists of a series of action scenes in interesting locations punctuated by brief, peaceful interludes in which the characters discuss how likely they are to encounter an otherworldly force on their quest. The camera is constantly in motion, the editing is quick, the sound design lends credibility to the movie's many foreign, period locales, and the score carries us lightly from scene to scene. When the supernatural forces finally reveal themselves, the movie adopts horror conventions—the scene takes place in a remote location, our heroes are bound and helpless, religious symbols are included prominently, the set lighting is harsh, the lights in the scene flicker and then go out, and the sounds of wind, screaming, and other unexplainable sounds dominate the soundtrack.

What do the genre conventions of *Raiders of the Lost Ark* suggest to us about the world? What can we learn solely from the film's cinematography, editing, sound design, and score without giving attention to its story at all?

In *Raiders of the Lost Ark*, quick, clever reactions are better than prudent forethought. Keep moving or die. One place is the same as any other. Local citizenry is either hostile or ambivalent. A life of adventure is never boring. There are powers at work in the world we don't understand. Those powers are on the side of good, and those powers cannot be stopped.

Casting

The relationship between actors and audience is a curious one. Unlike in live theater, the movie audience watches the actor, but the actor is unaware of the audience. We aren't present with actors. We only gaze upon them, and when that actor appears in another movie, we gaze upon them again. So, with few exceptions, a movie actor does not become enveloped in her or his role. Rather, the actor envelops the role, and the actor brings more to their roles in movies than simply their abilities to portray their characters with skill. They bring their screen personas as well.

So, whether we are watching *Top Gun* or *Jerry Maguire* or *Magnolia*, we are watching Tom Cruise give up his pride in favor of real love. Whether we're watching *High Noon* or

Rear Window or *High Society*, we are watching Grace Kelly step out of a life of safety and into adventure. We watch Tom Hanks try to get home from the far side of the moon in *Apollo 13*, listen to Tom Hanks bicker with Buzz Lightyear as they try to get home in *Toy Story*, and laugh at Tom Hanks as he dances on a giant piano and learns there's no better place than home in *Big*.

Sometimes actors play against type, and their screen persona is still an essential part of understanding what a movie is saying. When Henry Fonda dons a black hat to play a very bad man in *Once Upon A Time in the West*, it matters that he was known as the paragon of 1950s virtue. We recognize Tony Hale as the outrageously goofy Buster Bluth on *Arrested Development*, so when we watch him play a mild-mannered, nice man in Lauralee Farrer's indie gem *Not That Funny*, we see more clearly that a nice, normal guy can be attractive, too.

Since the actors are the ones who embody the character change the movie's story exists to show, the actors are what we connect to most strongly on the screen. We identify things about ourselves in them. We see our own ambition and search for love in Tom Cruise. We are as fearful as Grace Kelly and as thrilled by adventure. Like Tom Hanks, we long for home. As Stanley Cavall writes in his foundational text *The World Viewed*, "The creation of a (screen) performer is also the creation of a character—not the kind of character the author creates, but the kind that certain real people are: a type."[4] Identifying an actor's frequent type is a good way to understand what a movie is trying to say.

Harrison Ford's persona is one of "charming cockiness." He brings that same persona to other roles whether he's the President of the United States in *Air Force One*, a CIA analyst in *Patriot Games*, or a millionaire playboy in

4. Cavall, *The World Viewed*, 29.

Sabrina. Cocky and charming have become harder for Ford to sell as he has gotten older—wisdom, something we associate with age, and cockiness, the pride of youth, aren't complimentary characteristics—but he still manages to make his persona work from time to time, as in the underappreciated *Morning Glory*, where he plays a veteran news anchor with a chip on his shoulder and in *42*, where his cockiness was a perfect match for maverick baseball team owner Branch Rickey.

When we watch Indiana Jones fight Nazis on a moving truck in *Raiders of the Lost Ark*, we're not just watching a character named "Indiana Jones" do these things. We're watching Harrison Ford as Indiana Jones do these things. His persona is part of the character and essential to what a movie is saying—"Cockiness gets you nowhere. You have to do something for someone else to find happiness."

Questions to Ask During the Rising Action

1) What opportunities does the main character pass up to learn her or his lesson?

2) How does the movie tell its story? What is the movie's storytelling method?

3) How do the movie's cinematography, editing, and sound design contribute to its story?

4) What does the film's score want you to feel?

5) What are the actors feeling about what is happening in the story?

6) What is this film's genre?

7) What is typical of films in that genre?

8) How does this film adhere to or stray from that genre?

9) Do those things work? Why or why not?

10) What does the way this film uses those genre conventions tell us about humanity and the world?

11) Are these actors known for playing certain types of characters?

12) What might those types of characters tell us about the kind of movie this is?

THE CLIMAX AND RESOLUTION

The final fifteen to twenty minutes of a typical movie make up the *climax* and the *resolution*. In many movies, you can identify a single moment near the end of the film as the climax and everything that comes after as the resolution. In some movies, especially older movies, the climax is followed by the briefest of resolutions. We're left to imagine most of the resolution on our own.

Climax

The *climax* is the moment when the protagonists finally catch up to whatever they are chasing and have the option to either obtain it or let it go. In order to mature, the characters have to face their fears, choose to accept and embrace the things they have been running from, and let the things they have been chasing after get away. In doing so, they grow as people, and whatever else happens in the movie, the ending is happy. If the characters go ahead and take the things they have been chasing, abandoning the things they have been running from, they forfeit whatever emotional growth was possible, and the ending is tragic.

In *Raiders of the Lost Ark*, there are actually two climaxes. In the first, Indy mounts a rocket launcher on his shoulder and yells at Belloq to either drop the Ark or he'll blow it up along with everyone else, including himself and Marion. This is his last-ditch effort to get the Ark. Indy doesn't blow-up the Ark, not because he doesn't want a historical object to be destroyed as Belloq suggests, but because he doesn't want to lose Marion. He looks at her before he puts down the rocket launcher. Since before the movie began, Indiana Jones has been running from relationships in pursuit of his career. In the end, he chooses a woman over one of the greatest archaeological finds of all time.

In the second climax, Indiana Jones's other conflict comes to the fore. The Nazis have tied Indy and Marion to a post at the back of the canyon. Belloq and the Nazis are opening the Ark of the Covenant. The Nazis lift the lid and look inside. All they find is sand. The moment is a neat callback to the beginning of the film when Indiana Jones substitutes a bag of sand for a Peruvian god causing the temple around him to come to life and try to kill him. Belloq is dismayed; Indy smirks smugly, feeling vindicated in his disbelief. Then the Ark begins to glow, Indiana realizes his mistake, and responds humbly, closing his eyes and telling Marion to do the same. Closing his eyes is essential. Indiana Jones is a character whose deeper desire is to discover truth in the form of archaeological artifacts. Shutting his eyes isn't an explicit confession of newfound faith in God, but Indy does at least embrace ambiguity and accept his ignorance. This completes his character arc. He matures.

Raiders of the Lost Ark's ending is happy. For an example of a tragic ending, we'll look at *The Godfather*. If you haven't seen *The Godfather*, you should skip the next two paragraphs until you do.

Michael Corleone is a character who desires power. Salvation for Michael looks like embracing innocence and defending the weak. His first step down his tragic path is a noble one—seeing his father vulnerable and helpless in the hospital, Michael decides to involve himself in the family business in order to protect his father. Two scenes later, he has shifted from defending the weak to enacting vengeance, opting to kill rival gangster Sollozzo and the corrupt cop, McCluskey. Hiding out in Sicily, he encounters innocence again in the form of Apollonia, whom he marries. When she is taken from him by a car bomb, he returns home set on gaining as much power as possible to guarantee no one he loves is ever taken from him again.

The climax of *The Godfather* is the famous christening scene in which Michael settles all scores and consolidates the family business by murdering everyone that stands between him and what he wants. These killings are intercut with the christening of Michael's god-son. The scene is potent because of the score, the editing, and the violence depicted, but it's also powerful thematically, because Michael is standing in the presence of pure innocence, a baby being dedicated to God in a church, as his henchmen enact his final rejection of innocence outside the church. Presented with innocence, Michael chooses power, and his ending is tragic.

Resolution

A movie's *resolution* is the wrap-up. It shows what happens after the character makes her or his decision. Subplots that haven't already been resolved are resolved, and the movie either ends or sets the audience up for a sequel. Often, after the characters have let the things they were chasing go and have chosen maturity instead, they get the things after all. Indiana Jones gets the Ark, sort of, and the girl, in addition to learning to put people before work and to allow for something beyond his understanding. In a tragedy, the character might get the thing, but she or he loses everything else in the process.

Questions to Ask During the Climax and Resolution

1) When does everything seem most hopeless?

2) What is required of the character for her or him to get out of the predicament?

3) How does the character respond? How is this response different than how she or he has responded throughout the rest of the movie?

4) What does the character learn?

5) What is different in the character's life when the movie ends compared to when it began?

6

NOW, RESPOND

Now that we have listened to a movie, it is our turn to respond.

We've allowed the movie to bring up themes, ideas, topics, and questions about the world, humanity's place in it and responsibility to it and to each other. Maybe the movie even explored God's activity in the world and in our lives. Maybe the movie offered some opinions on those matters. Maybe it simply asked and explored the questions. In any case, we've allowed the movie to set the terms of the conversation. It is good that we have done this. It is a humble, hospitable, gracious way to interact with a work of art that is the result of thousands of hours of passion-fueled, human work. By listening first, we've earned the right and prepared ourselves well to respond.

The first question most people ask each other after a movie ends is, "Did you like it?" The marketing for movies wants us to ask that question. We're told by bus stops and billboards and commercial breaks and banner ads on websites that we will "like" every movie made. To bring us pleasure becomes, in the marketing and in our minds, the reason for every movie's existence.

Liking or not liking a movie can be a good place to begin a conversation with (and about) a movie, but the conversation should not end there. We need to push beyond like and dislike and begin to ask *why* we like or dislike a movie. What is a movie doing that we like? What do we dislike? Why do we like or dislike those things? We need to ask what those likes and dislikes might say about us, not just what they say about the movie. As in interacting with other people, liking or disliking a movie is not an excuse to either blindly accept it and what it has to say or to dismiss it entirely. Love, expressed as respect for the people who made the movie, requires us to interact with the movie whether we like it or not.

Instead of merely thinking about whether or not we like the movie, take note of the words, images, moments, and ideas that most linger with you after the movie ends. Ask what those things mean in the context of the story. We can ask ourselves, "Does the Bible use any of those same words, images, story beats, or ideas?" If so, what does the Bible say about those things? We can ask ourselves, "Have I experienced anything similar in my own life, and how has God used those experiences to mature my faith?" We can look for ways in which the movie's characters' struggles reflect our own struggles. Did the characters respond wisely? How does the Bible and the work of God's Spirit in our lives suggest they should have responded? The characters won't always respond wisely, just as we don't always respond wisely to similar situations in our lives. We need to both affirm what is good in a movie and humbly question what is not good.

As we do this, we are bringing our faith to the movie in a way that does not constrict the movie or our experience of it, but rather opens up the movie to the complexities of real life and opens us up to the living activity of God's Spirit in our lives and in the world. We are looking in the movie and in ourselves for the "good" and "perfect" gift that comes "from above" (James 1:17). We are allowing the movie to push us deeper into God's Word. First we watch the movie. Then, we take the issues the movie raises and "study the perfect law, the law of freedom, and continue to do it" (James 1:25).

Finally, just as the characters in the movie did something that demonstrated the change that had taken place in them over the course of the film, we need to do something in response to what God shows us through the film. It is not enough to merely listen and respond. We must put what God has shown us "into practice in their lives," and then we "will be blessed in whatever [we] do" (James 1:25). Perhaps we'll need to subtly change the way we think about something, someone, or a situation in our lives. Perhaps a prayer of confession will be in order. Perhaps we'll need to forgive someone. Perhaps we'll be encouraged to stop behaving a certain way. Perhaps we'll be inspired to start doing something good we've never done before. Whatever the case, we must take what we have learned by talking to a movie and put it into action in our lives.

Questions to Ask After the Movie Ends

1) What do I like or dislike about this movie?

2) What does the way this movie affected me suggest about me and about the movie?

3) What does the film critique? What does it value?

4) How does it attempt to demonstrate this? Are its methods successful?

5) What does my Christian faith say about that same issue?

6) How do the film and my faith agree and disagree?

7) How can I apply this to my life? How might this inspire me toward greater worship of God and love of the world?

7

AN EXERCISE—TALK TO TOY STORY

Below, I've provided the chance for you to have a conversation with one of the most popular films of all time—*Toy Story*. You should try to answer the questions yourself without looking at my answers. My answers are included for your reference in an appendix. Your answers might differ from mine. That's okay. While we do try to hear definitively what a movie is saying, works of art are complicated, and you might hear differently from me. Your final answers responding to *Toy Story* will almost certainly differ from mine, as God is doing a unique work in your life.

PROBLEM

1) Who is the main character?
2) How do you know?

3) What is he or she chasing or trying to accomplish? What does he or she want?

4) Why is he or she chasing it?

5) What negative character trait does chasing this thing reveal?

6) What positive character trait does he or she need instead?

7) What does he or she need to do to achieve that positive character trait?

RISING ACTION

1) What does the character do to try to get the thing she or he wants?

2) What kinds of filmmaking techniques does the film employ to show this?

3) What does the story look like? What is its genre?

4) What is typical of films in that genre?

5) What might we expect about how this film will resolve based on its genre?

6) How can the techniques of that genre be used in positive and negative ways?

7) What does the way this film uses its genre characteristics communicate to us about people and the world?

8) Are these actors known for playing certain types of characters?

9) What might those types of characters tell us about the kind of movie this is?

CLIMAX AND RESOLUTION

1) At what point is the main character most hopeless?

2) What object or dream has she or he given up ever attaining at that point?

3) What negative thing has she or he discovered about themselves and/or the world?

4) What happens that pulls him or her out of hopelessness?

5) What new hope does she or he discover?

6) What positive character trait(s) does this new hope represent?

7) How does the story resolve? What images are most prominent?

FINAL REVIEW

1) What does the film critique? What does it value?

2) How does it attempt to demonstrate this? Are its methods successful?

3) What does your Christian faith say about that same issue?

4) How do the film and your faith agree and disagree?

5) How can you apply this to your life? How might this inspire you toward greater worship of God and love of the world?

PUTTING IT ALL TOGETHER

Summarize all your answers to the questions in few paragraphs that concisely communicates what you heard in the movie and how you want to apply it to your life. Again, you can read my final reflection on *Toy Story* in the appendix for an example of how you might do this.

8

CONCLUSION—FOUR CONVERSATIONS WITH FOUR FILMMAKERS

ADJUST YOUR EXPECTATIONS

Have you seen *The Adjustment Bureau*? The high-concept, science-fiction, romance, adventure film starring Matt Damon and Emily Blunt as a pair of would-be lovers kept apart by a team of mysterious, bowler hat-wearing, reality-adjusting men was a difficult sell for marketers, but it has developed somewhat of a cult following in the years since its release. Reel Spirituality, the group I work and write for at Fuller Theological Seminary, was given the chance to host a pre-screening of the film for our community of pastors and future Christian leaders. After the film, Rob Johnston led the audience in a group discussion about the curious interplay between God's divine will and humanity's supposed free will—a discussion that arises naturally from the film. The discussion was lively. The audience seemed to have a great time.

One person in the audience was particularly invigorated by the discussion—the writer/director of the film, George Nolfi. He was there secretly to see how a "religious audience" would respond to his film. He was so thrilled by our theological discussion, he offered us a second pre-screening of the film if we were willing to gather representatives from each of the world's major monotheistic religions—Judaism, Islam, and Christianity—so that he could have that same discussion with those religious leaders. He made the movie, because he wanted to talk about the mysterious relationship between fate and free will. We provided a context for that discussion.

Since then, Johnston regularly assigns *The Adjustment Bureau* in his yearly Theology and Film class, and George Nolfi has attended the class to have that discussion again with each year's students. Our pre-screening of *The Adjustment Bureau* prompted the film's director to adjust his expectations of the way audiences were capable of interacting with his film; his presence in Johnston's class prompts students to adjust their expectations of what filmmakers hope to accomplish with their films.

George Nolfi is an exceptional example, but he is evidence that filmmakers make films because they want to talk about the things their films are about. Talking to a movie isn't just a better way to watch a movie. It's what many filmmakers hope you'll do.

FLOODED WITH CONTROVERSY

Have you seen *Noah*? During *Noah*'s promotional tour, my work as a film critic for Reel Spirituality garnered me and my colleague, Kutter Callaway, the chance to participate in a round-table interview with Darren Aronofsky and Ari Handel, the writer/director and writer, respectively, of the controversial 2014 film. Aronofsky and Handel's adaptation of the biblical tale raised the ire of many Christians prior to the film's release because of the liberties they supposedly took with the story—allegedly turning God's righteous shipbuilder into a vegetarian environmentalist with a penchant for child abuse. Some Christians feared a "biblically inaccurate" big screen version of the Flood narrative would confuse audiences or, worse, convince them of an alternate, unorthodox reading of the text.

Their fears were unfounded. While Aronofsky and Handel's take on the story was certainly fantastic and a product of its time—*Noah* looks and feels more like *The Lord of the Rings* than it does *The Ten Commandments*—the filmmakers exhibited a faithfulness to the details present in the biblical text that ought to make even the most dogged fundamentalist blush. The liberties they took were only with regards to the more ambiguous portions of the Genesis passage or when they needed to fill in the gaps to make the story "live," and in each case, what they imagined to fill those gaps proved visually and thematically compelling. Casting their Nephilim as angels who fell so in love with humanity that they abandoned heaven and became caged in earth was particularly brilliant. The Nephilim's eventual reconciliation with God is one of the film's most powerful moments, foreshadowing the rainbowed reconciliation to come between God and humanity.

That was just one example of Aronofsky and Handel's creativity in adapting this story for contemporary audiences. It was clear to me that they had spent more time thinking about this story than most people ever have. I hoped that our round-table interview would focus more on their compelling, creative way of telling this story and on the questions that drove their research and less on the controversy surrounding it. But, of course, controversy sells better than creativity, so while many of the other journalists' questions honored the film, some of them continued to court the controversy. Aronofsky and Handel dealt with their concerns well. My favorite of Aronofsky's responses to the questions about accuracy was the following. He said, "It's more powerful being symbolic of all these ideas that are in [the Noah story]—of original sin and what it does—and if you can unleash that mythical power of these stories and of these characters, you can inspire a lot more, and you can learn from it in a lot of ways. It makes it a living text as opposed to just a question of accuracy."

Finally, at the end of the interview, Callaway had a chance to ask a question, and he took the opportunity to apologize to the filmmakers for any grief Christians had caused them over the past year as they made their film and prepared to show it to the world. Callaway said,

> I represent and work for "the largest Evangelical seminary in the world," so we connect with a lot of people who were in the "We hate *Noah*" crowd . . . and after hearing your hearts and seeing the movie, I just feel like it's the most God-affirming, faith-affirming, Creation-affirming movie I've seen in a long time, and I can't speak for all of Evangelicalism, but I just want to say "I'm sorry." I'm serious.

Afterwards, the publicists working for the film told us that Callaway's apology had meant a lot to the filmmakers, because they had suffered a lot from the hatred they had experienced coming from Christians.

In our increasingly connected age, the way we respond to movies matters. What we say about their movies flows back up the publicity pipeline to filmmakers. There is great potential in this new dynamic to create cooperative relationships between filmmakers and fans. There is great danger in this new dynamic as well, if we use our power to spew hatred instead of communicating love. How we behave doesn't only affect others. Our behavior affects our own souls as well. We need to respond lovingly to movies so that we continue to learn to love better in every circumstance. Talking to a movie is a way to practice loving well.

THE GOOD MAN

Have you seen *Calvary*? The Reel Spirituality community of filmmakers and film scholars voted it our Film of the Year in 2014 for both its theological depth and cinematic eloquence. *Calvary* begins in a confessional where a good priest, Father James, is surprised to learn that one of his parishioners was molested as a young boy by another priest, now deceased. The parishioner then tells Father James that in a week, on Sunday morning, he's going to kill Father James as a way of making the Catholic church atone for the bad priest's sin. *Calvary* follows Father James over the next week as he makes his rounds, argues with parishioners who are angry at God and the Church for a variety of reasons, and tries to decide what to do about the situation. For Christians, and especially Christian ministers, engaged daily with people who are antagonistic to our faith for reasons similar to those embodied by the parishioners in the film, Father James is a cinematic beacon of the faithful, penitent, humble, strong love that best witnesses to Christ's work in our lives. We watch his walk to Calvary and are humbled ourselves.

Calvary's Father James is played by Brendan Gleeson, the bear of a man who you may know best from his roles as

Hamish in *Braveheart* or Professor "Mad Eye" Moody in the *Harry Potter* series of films. He's not a "marquee name" like Tom Hanks or Julia Roberts. He's a working actor who takes the roles he can get. Every once in a while he gets to carry a film as in *Calvary*, *The Guard*, *The General*, or in *Into the Storm*, the HBO film about Winston Churchill for which Gleeson won a Prime Time Emmy for Outstanding Lead Performance in a Miniseries or Movie. I admire Gleeson, because there's an integrity inherent in not being a star, taking the work you can get, giving it your all, and excelling in the station God has placed you in life.

Studying his career, I see a similar integrity in many of the characters he has portrayed. As I covered in our discussion of acting earlier in this book, actors tend toward certain types of characters. Gleeson tends toward characters who adhere to a strict, personal, moral code. Walter Cahill in *The General*, "Monk" McGinn in *Gangs of New York*, August Nicholson in *The Village*, Ken in *In Bruges*, Abbot Celiach in *The Secret of Kells*, Winston Churchill in *Into the Storm*, Martin Brown in *Green Zone*, Gerry Boyle in *The Guard*, Father James in *Calvary*, and yes, even "Mad Eye" Moody in the *Harry Potter* movies are all characters who are committed to their understanding of what is right, and they frequently die in defense of it. They may not always be the most law-abiding men, but what is right and honorable often transcends human laws. Many of Brendan Gleeson's characters are honorable to a fault.

Or at least I thought they were. You never really know unless you have the chance to ask the person responsible for giving those characters life on screen. I got that chance during *Calvary*'s publicity tour in a brief phone interview. I began by asking Gleeson, "You seem to like playing characters with a strong sense of right and wrong, and that sense seems to often differ from the culture around them. . .

They're like iconoclasts. Do you seek out those roles purposefully, and if so, why do you enjoy playing those kinds of characters?"

"Yeah," Gleeson replied, "I certainly try to access the particular set of morals a particular character has without assuming that, because they mightn't be the general morals, they're not heartfelt. Sometimes people just do things because they do things—it's their job or whatever—but a lot of the time I try to find the rationale for people, what would lead them to figure that it's okay for them to act in a particular way, whether that's a villainous way or whether it's someone who's committed to 'keeping the flame alight.'"

Gleeson has certainly played a lot of villainous characters, but he said he always tries to find the good in them, that moral rationale that motivates their villainous deeds. He said he enjoyed playing Father James precisely because his commitment to God is clear. "It was interesting to play someone who nails his colors to the mast," Gleeson said, "and stands by them."

Father James's commitment to stay committed in the face of impending death makes him have more in common with a Western hero than a typical theologian. I asked Gleeson if that was an intentional reference and, if so, if he saw Father James as more of a Gary Cooper or John Wayne Western hero.

"Certainly *High Noon*. [Father James] goes around trying to absorb his parishioners' pain. I can't imagine John Wayne doing that," Gleeson replied. "I think [Father James] is more physically afraid in a way that Gary Cooper seemed to be easy with. [Gary Cooper] wasn't afraid to show fear on screen. John Wayne did less of that. For me it would have been more *High Noon* than *The Searchers*." Gleeson also cited Trevor Howard's performance as Father Collins in David Lean's film *Ryan's Daughter* as an influence on his performance.

Gleeson also mentioned *Ryan's Daughter's* cinematography as an influence on *Calvary's* cinematography. In David Lean's epics, the landscape says much about the people living in it and what they are feeling. *Calvary's* Irish coast is raw, tempestuous, and imposing just like the people Father James encounters and just like Father James himself. And just as David Lean's epics are as much about the Arabian peninsula, Russia, Ireland, and India as they are about the people shaped by those places, so *Calvary* is as much about Ireland's response to the recent sexual abuse scandals in the Catholic church as it is about this one good man falsely condemned.

When you watch *Calvary*, you can enjoy it without knowing about Brendan Gleeson's former roles. You don't have to recognize *Calvary's* genre-resemblance to Westerns (particularly *High Noon*), or it's visual and tonal references to David Lean's film, *Ryan's Daughter*, but that is the way the filmmakers behind *Calvary* talk about their film. The acting, genre, and cinematography are the language *Calvary* speaks. Understanding them better and knowing what to look for adds another layer of meaning to an already meaningful film.

FATHERS AND SONS

Have you seen *Last Days in the Desert*? The film is about Jesus as he is leaving the wilderness following his forty days of fasting and praying prior to beginning his ministry. The writer/director, Rodrigo Garcia, realized there was a little gap in the biblical narrative that he could use to create a Jesus story without having to mind all the details contained in the Gospels. Garcia imagined Jesus encountering a family who lives in the desert and the ways Jesus' preparation for ministry might overlap with the relationship between the father, mother, and son in the family. *Last Days in the Desert* is a simple, beautiful film that asks thoughtful questions about what it means to be a father, what it means to be a son, and the responsibilities fathers and sons have to each other.

I've seen the movie seven times now, and each time it has left me thinking about my own relationship with my father. I am blessed to be able to say that my father and I have a great relationship. There's no friction, and I genuinely look forward to spending time with him. I have great respect for him, and I know he loves and respects me too.

But at times in my life, I have wondered what my father expects of me. Because I admire him, I want to please him. I want to do the things he wants me to do. When I was in high school preparing to go to college and "make something of my life," I longed for my dad to just tell me what to do, to lay out a plan for my life that would fit me and that would please him. He never did that. To his credit, he allowed me to pursue Christ and discern God's will for my life on my own. He was there if I needed him, but he didn't force his will on me. It took me a long time to understand that and to be grateful for it.

In *Last Days in the Desert*, Jesus and the boy he meets are both struggling with their fathers' will for their lives. Jesus is trying to discern it; and the teenage boy is fighting against it. Both are looking for their fathers to commend them and bless their missions in life. Neither son gets his father to do that. Both fathers stay silent, just as my father was silent about my mission in life when I was growing up. There is resolution in *Last Days in the Desert* though—I won't spoil it for you—but it helped me understand my own father's silence.

Every year at Sundance, Fuller Seminary participates in the Windrider Forum, a gathering of theologically-interested movie-watchers who go to Sundance films together and meet daily to talk with each other and occasionally with filmmakers about the movies they are seeing. In 2015 when *Last Days in the Desert* premiered at the festival, on behalf of the Windrider Forum, I had a chance to interview Rodrigo Garcia about his film. Naturally, I brought up the way *Last Days in the Desert* has helped me understand my father's silence concerning my calling in life.

"Of course [God] has to be silent [with Jesus]," Garcia exclaimed, "The mission is so big, the destiny is so huge, that as a father, I would not want my son to debate me on this. It's like, 'This is the mission. You can do it. We're done talking.' Do you know what I mean? I'm not talking from a theological point of view. As a father/son thing, if I don't talk to you, you'll be able to do it."

That is exactly right. My own father had taught me my entire life that my mission was to be sensitive to the Spirit, to follow Christ by taking that next step of faith, and to be content with where God placed me. As I prepared to step out of our home and into the rest of my life, there was nothing more to say. Everything important had already been said. I just needed to follow the simple instruction I'd already been given.

Last Days in the Desert helped me find final peace with my father's silence regarding my mission in life. The movie prompted me to let go of any disappointment or frustration I was still harboring toward my father. The movie gave me new purpose in following Christ and a new joy to know I was doing exactly what my father and my Heavenly Father wanted.

CONCLUSION

Unless you become a movie journalist, you likely won't find yourself in regular conversations with filmmakers, but you can still talk to their movies. Talking to a movie is a better way to watch a movie, because doing so honors the movie and the filmmakers behind it. Talking to a movie is the way many filmmakers want you to interact with their films.

Once again, it is also a more Christ-like way to interact with movies, because it is a more hospitable way to interact with films and the women and men who make them. For too long Christians have responded to movies with hostility and most often without actually seeing the movies first. Rather than getting upset with films and filmmakers because of what we think they are saying, talking to a movie positions us to listen to what the movie is actually saying. Then, when we respond, we do so out of love and not out of fear.

Because talking to a movie involves learning to speak the movie's language of cinematography, editing, sound design, scoring, genre, and acting, talking to a movie is a way to get more out of movie than if we just passively watch them. We will understand the movies better, and we'll discover more ways the movie's story and our stories are the same.

Ultimately, talking to a movie makes us more aware of what God is doing in the world and in our lives. It helps us know what we are supposed to do to love ourselves, each other, and the world better. If we do this consistently, and if we put into practice in our lives what God says to us through the movies, talking to a movie becomes a kind of spiritual discipline. Movie-watching can be tool God uses to make us more like Christ.

APPENDIX
Talking to *Toy Story*

Below are my answers to the questions I listed for you to answer while watching and after watching *Toy Story*. Once again, if your answers differ from mine, that's okay as long as what you hear from the movie is supported by the movie's method.

PROBLEM

1) *Who is the main character?* Woody.

2) *How do you know?* Almost everything we see revolves around him and his experience.

3) *What is he or she chasing or trying to accomplish? What does he or she want?* He wants to be Andy's favorite toy again.

4) *Why is he or she chasing it?* He loves to be loved by Andy.

5) *What negative character trait does chasing this thing reveal?* It reveals Woody's pride in being Andy's favorite toy.

6) *What positive character trait does he or she need instead?* Woody needs to learn humility, to value Andy's love even if Woody isn't Andy's favorite, and to be a good toy regardless.

7) *What does he or she need to do to achieve that positive character trait?* Woody needs to accept his new role in the room and to be nice to Buzz.

RISING ACTION

1) *What does the character do to try to get the thing she or he wants?* Woody tries to reveal Buzz's stupidity to the rest of the toys, and then he tries to knock Buzz behind the dresser.

2) *What kinds of filmmaking techniques does the film employ to show this?* Cinematography: Woody is frequently shown disgustedly watching Buzz do things for the other toys. Editing: A montage scene set to music shows Woody being replaced by Buzz.

3) *What does the story look like? What is its genre?* Woody and Buzz go on a journey together to try and get home. *Toy Story* is a Buddy Comedy.

4) *What is typical of films in that genre?* Two people who don't get along with each other because they are very different learn to appreciate each other and become friends.

5) *What might we expect about how this film will resolve based on its genre?* Woody will probably learn to appreciate Buzz and will be willing to abandon his other goals in favor of helping Buzz. Buzz's quirks will prove invaluable for accomplishing what Woody wants to accomplish.

6) *How can the techniques of that genre be used in positive and negative ways?* If the movie makes fun of the weird person by stereotyping them in some way, that's negative. If the movie uses Buddy Comedy techniques to help us appreciate normally marginalized people, that's positive. Buddy Comedy techniques could also be used positively to encourage us to value others especially when they seem odd to us.

7) *What does the way this film uses its genre characteristics communicate to us about people and the world?* There is space for everyone. People have gifts and talents that may not be obvious at first. Everyone has a role to play. There is honor in all stations of life.

8) *Are these actors known for playing certain types of characters?* Tom Hanks often plays characters who don't want their peaceful lives upset and who struggle to get back home. That's what happens to Woody here. Tim Allen is known for playing good-natured, dim-witted characters who are a little too self-assured and have to learn to accept their limitations and be content with their place in life. That's certainly Buzz.

9) *What might those types of characters tell us about the kind of movie this is?* The character who just wants peace and the ambitious character are naturally going to be at odds, so this movie is probably about them coming to understand each other and value each other in their differences. We can also expect a journey and for Buzz to be humbled at some point.

APPENDIX

CLIMAX AND RESOLUTION

1) *At what point is the main character most hopeless?* Woody is most hopeless after the toys in Andy's room refuse to help him escape Sid's room. He thinks he'll never get home again.

2) *What object or dream has she or he given up ever attaining at that point?* Getting back to Andy, being loved by a kid, having a place where he fits in the world.

3) *What negative thing has she or he discovered about themselves and/or the world?* High-standing/status if fleeting. One moment you're on top of the world, and the next you're all but forgotten.

4) *What happens that pulls him or her out of hopelessness?* Buzz reminds Woody who he is made to be—Andy's toy—and decides to help them both get home.

5) *What new hope does she or he discover?* It is good to be loved even if you're not the "most loved," and love from friends is just as valuable as love from a kid.

6) *What positive character trait(s) does this new hope represent?* Humility, Gratefulness, Selflessness, Contentment

7) *How does the story resolve? What images are most prominent?* With the help of all the other toys in Sid's room and the Andy's toys in the moving truck, Woody and Buzz make it back to Andy's side. The image of Sid's toys confronting him is strong. So is the image of Buzz and Woody flying together through the air. In both, toys are helping each other, suggesting that only together can they fulfill their destinies of being loved by a kid, and they'll be happy together regardless.

FINAL REVIEW

1) *What does the film critique? What does it value? Toy Story* critiques pride and needing to be the favorite. *Toy Story* values humility and contentment.

2) *How does it attempt to demonstrate this? Are its methods successful?* The movie takes Woody from the top of the pile of toys to being content no matter his status. The movie is very successful.

3) *What does your Christian faith say about that same issue?* Our faith says that every person has a role to play in God's kingdom, and there is no more inherent value in any one role over the others. We are supposed to love all equally just as God does and not get caught up in trying to be seen as better than anyone else.

4) *How do the film and your faith agree and disagree?* Our faith and *Toy Story* say the same thing about how we are to relate to Divine authority and to each other.

5) *How can you apply this to your life? How might this inspire you toward greater worship of God and love of the world?* I need to be satisfied with the life and work God has given me without comparing myself to others. My "spot" in life is good, because God has placed me here, loves me, and is faithful to me. Yes, at times it may feel like I'm riding higher than at other times, but God's love is constant. God has written his name on my heart. I belong to God and should delight in that alone. Also, I should recognize the value of other people in my life and love them as God does, and especially when I'm tempted to be jealous of them. Maybe that person is "better off" than me, but compared to God, we're both at the same level. I ought to love others without prejudice, like God does.

PUTTING IT ALL TOGETHER

Toy Story tells the story of Woody (voiced by Tom Hanks), a toy who begins on top of the world, gets displaced to the bottom, and has to learn to be content no matter his status. Along the way he becomes friends with the toy who replaced him, Buzz (voiced by Tim Allen), and discovers that Buzz's quirks make Woody's life better, even though they annoy him at first. *Toy Story* is a road movie/buddy comedy where the characters end up back where they started having learned more about themselves and with greater appreciation for each other.

Toy Story is a computer animated film—the first of its kind, actually—and the filmmakers at Pixar take advantage of their ability to put a camera anywhere to communicate the story's idea primarily through the film's cinematography. Early in the film when the story is confined to Andy's room, Woody is shot from below or from close distances. This makes him appear large. He dominates the frame just as he dominates Andy's room. After Buzz arrives and they get ejected from the room into the greater world, Woody is small. He's "toy-sized" again. At the end of the film, when Woody and Buzz finally work together, they soar through the sky, bigger than life and triumphant.

Toy Story's score also plays a key role in communicating its story. A montage set to Randy Newman's "Strange Things" takes Woody from the top of the heap to the bottom in a collection of humorous scenes. "I Will Go Sailing No More" is a tragic song that accompanies Buzz's realization that he is only a toy, not a space ranger, though he learns to be content with that later. "You've Got A Friend In Me" serves as a bookend to the film, highlighting Woody and Andy's friendship in the beginning of the story and Woody and Buzz's friendship in the end.

Ultimately, *Toy Story* encourages us to be satisfied with our station in life regardless of where we are situated. Andy is like God to his toys. They base their sense of value on how he values them. Woody has to learn that Andy loves him regardless of whether or not Woody sees himself as Andy's "favorite" just as we need to learn to trust God's love for us even when it seems others are receiving more of God's favor. Woody also has to learn to love his fellow toys instead of lording his high status over them. We can benefit from this lesson as well as we seek to love our brothers and sisters in Christ better regardless of their perceived "value." Ultimately, God is far above us, and we are all equal in God's love.

BIBLIOGRAPHY

Callaway, Kutter. *Scoring Transcendence: Contemporary Film Music as Religious Experience.* Waco, TX: Baylor University Press, 2012.

Cavell, Stanley. *The World Viewed: Reflections on the Ontology of Film.* Cambridge, MA: Harvard University Press, 1979.

Ebert, Andreas, and Ricahrd Rohr. *The Enneagram: A Christian Perspective.* New York: Crossroad, 2001.

Hutzler, Laurie. *Emotional Toolbox Screenwriting.* September 2, 2015. Online: http://www.etbscreenwriting.com/.

Johnston, Robert. *God's Wider Presence: Reevaluating General Revelation.* Grand Rapids, MI: Baker Academic, 2014.

McKee, Robert. *Story: Style, Structure, Substance, and the Principles of Screenwriting.* New York: Regan, 1997.

Pigliucci, Massimo. *Answers for Aristotle: How Science and Philosophy Can Lead Us to a More Meaningful Life.* New York: Basic, 2012.

Pohl, Christine. *Making Room: Recovering Hospitality as a Christian Discipline.* Grand Rapids, MI: Eerdmans, 1999.

Tarkovsky, Andrey. *Sculpting in Time: Reflections on Cinema.* London: Bodley Head, 1986.

Taylor, Charles. *A Secular Age.* Cambridge, MA: Harvard, 2007.

FILMOGRAPHY

2001: A Space Odyssey. Dir. Stanley Kubrick. Metro-Goldwyn-Mayer, 1968.

42. Dir. Brian Helgeland. Warner Bros., 2013.

A Beautiful Mind. Dir. Ron Howard. Universal Pictures, 2001.

The Adjustment Bureau. Dir. George Nolfi. Universal Pictures, 2011.

Air Force One. Dir. Wolfgang Peterson. Columbia Pictures Corporation, 1997.

An Inconvenient Truth. Dir. Davis Guggenheim. Participant Media, 2006.

Apollo 13. Dir. Ron Howard. Universal Pictures, 1995.

Arrested Development. Creator Mitchell Hurwitz. 20th Century Fox Television, 2003.

Avatar. Dir. James Cameron. Twentieth Century Fox Film Corporation, 2009.

Babette's Feast. Dir. Gabriel Axel. Orion Classics, 1987.

Back to the Future. Dir. Robert Zemeckis. Universal Pictures, 1985.

Becoming Jane. Dir. Julian Jarrold. HanWay Films, 2007.

Big. Dir. Penny Marshall. Twentieth Century Fox Film Corporation, 1988.

Birdman: Or (The Unexpected Virtue of Ignorance). Dir. Alejandro G. Iñárritu. Fox Searchlight, 2014.

The Bourne Identity. Dir. Doug Liman. Universal Pictures, 2002.

Braveheart. Dir. Mel Gibson. Paramount Pictures, 1995.

Calvary. Dir. John Michael McDonagh. Fox Searchlight Pictures, 2014.

Cast Away. Dir. Robert Zebecks. Twentieth Century Fox Film Corporation, 2000.

Chinatown. Dir. Roman Polanski. Paramount Pictures, 1974.

The Dot and the Line: A Romance in Lower Mathematics. Dir. Chuck Jones. Metro-Goldwyn-Meyer, 1965.

Citizen Kane. Dir. Orson Wells. RKO Radio Pictures, 1941.

Daughters of the Dust. Dir. Julie Dash. Kino international, 1991.

Gangs of New York. Dir. Martin Scorsese. Miramax, 2002.

The General. Dir. John Boorman. Sony Pictures Classics, 1998.

Gladiator. Dir. Ridley Scott. Universal Pictures, 2000.

The Godfather. Dir. Francis Ford Coppola. Paramount Pictures, 1972.

Green Zone. Dir. Paul Greengrass. Universal Pictures, 2010.

Groundhog Day. Dir. Harold Ramis. Columbia Pictures Corporation, 1993.

The Guard. Dir. John Michael McDonagh. Sony Pictures Classics, 2011.

Harry Potter (series). Dir. various. Warner Bros., 2005–2001.

High Noon. Dir. Fred Zinnemann. United Artists, 1952.

High Society. Dir. Charles Walters. Metro-Goldwyn-Meyer, 1956.

The Hobbit (series). Dir. Peter Jackson. Newline Cinema, 2012.

The Imitation Game. Dir. Morton Tyldum. The Weinstein Company, 2014.

In Bruges. Dir. Martin McDonagh. Focus Features, 2008.

Into the Storm. Dir. Thaddeus O'Sullivan. HBO Films, 2008.

Intolerance: Love's Struggle Throughout the Ages. Dir. D.W. Griffith. Triangle Distributing, 1916.

Jerry Maguire. Dir. Cameron Crowe. TriStar Pictures, 1996.

Joe Versus the Volcano. Dir, John Patrick Shanley. Warner Bros., 1990.

Juno. Dir. Jason Reitman. Fox Searchlight, 2007.

Last Days in the Desert. Dir. Rodrigo Garcia. Mockingbird Pictures, 2016.

Magnolia. Dir. Paul Thomas Anderson. New Line Cinema, 1999.

Mean Girls. Dir. Mark Waters. Paramount Pictures, 2004.

Mission: Impossible. Dir. Brian De Palma. Paramount Pictures, 1996.

Morning Glory. Dir. Roger Michell. Paramount Pictures, 2010.

Nightcrawler. Dir. Dan Gilroy. Open Road Films, 2014.

Noah. Dir. Darren Aronofsky. Paramount Pictures, 2012.

Not That Funny. Dir. Lauralee Farrer. Boulevard Pictures, 2012.

Ocean's Eleven. Dir. Steven Soderbergh. Warner Bros., 2001.

Once Upon A Time in the West. Dir. Sergio Leone. Paramount Pictures, 1968.

Patriot Games. Dir. Phillip Noyce. Paramount Pictures, 1992.

Pollock. Dir. Ed Harris. Sony Pictures Classics, 2000.

The Purple Rose of Cairo. Dir. Woody Allen. Orion Pictures, 1985.

Raiders of the Lost Ark. Dir. Steven Spielberg. Paramount Pictures, 1981.

Ratatouille. Dirs. Brad Bird and Jan Pinkava. The Walt Disney Company, 2007.

Rear Window. Dir. Alfred Hitchcock. Paramount Pictures, 1954.

Ryan's Daughter. Dir. David Lean. Metro-Goldwyn-Meyer, 1970.

Sabrina. Dir. Sydney Pollack. Paramount Pictures, 1995.

Saving Private Ryan. Dir. Steven Spielberg. Dreamwork's Distribution, 1998.

School Daze. Dir. Spike Lee. Columbia Pictures, 1988.

The Searchers. Dir. John Ford. Warner Bros., 1956.

The Secret of Kells. Dirs. Tomm Moore and Nora Twomey. Canal+, 2009.

Shane. Dir. George Stevens. Paramount Pictures, 1953.

Sherlock Jr.. Dir. Buster Keaton. Metro Pictures Corporation, 1924.

Skyfall. Dir. Sam Mendes. Sony Pcitures, 2012.

Space Jam. Dir. Joe Pytka. Warner Bros. Family Entertainment, 1996.

Taxi Driver. Dir. Martin Scorsese. Columbia Pictures Corporation, 1976.

Timbuktu. Dir. Abderrahmane Sissako. Cohen Media Group, 2014.

Top Gun. Dir. Tony Scott. Paramount Pictures, 1986.

Toy Story. Dir. John Lasseter. Buena Vista Pictures, 1995.

Vertigo. Dir. Alfred Hitchcock. Paramount Pictures, 1958.

The Village. Dir. M. Night Shyamalan. Touchstone Pictures, 2004.

WALL•E. Dir. Andrew Stanton. Walt Disney Pictures, 2008.

Wayne's World. Dir. Penelope Spheeris. Paramount Pictures, 1992.

The Wolf of Wall Street. Dir. Martin Scorsese. Paramount Pictures, 2013.

Zero Dark Thirty. Dir. Kathryn Bigelow. Columbia Pictures, 2012.